My Outrageous!

Spiritual Adventure

(Spiritual Initiations)

by

Kevin Michael

Book design by Kevin Michael

Kevin Michael books are available for order through Ingram Press Catalogues

Some of the names in this book have been changed to protect the privacy of individuals.

Visit my website at www.kevinmichael.net
Kevin Michael and Vidya Training Services LLC

Printed in the United States of America
First Printing: August 2016
Published by Sojourn Publishing, LLC

ISBN: 978-1-62747-222-7
Ebook ISBN: 978-1-62747-223-4

Dedication

This work is dedicated to my primary spiritual teacher,

Sathya Sai Baba of Puttaparthi, India

Contents

Introduction

At various places in this book, you will find text in italics. The commentary shown in italics represents the author's interpretive and directive notes, given to facilitate the use of the material for the reader.

Introducing the Bridgers

The Bridgers are members of ascended humanity who themselves have been through the human evolution. They know what it is like. They know about suffering. They know how it feels to live lives here on planet Earth. They have given themselves in service to those who choose to ask for their help. There will be more about the Bridgers and the Bridging process as you go further into this book.

~

Chapter 1
Awakenings

"Yesterday I was clever,
so I wanted to change the world.
Today I am wise,
So I am changing myself."

-Rumi

Archangel Michael Awakening Event

It happened at dawn on a cold Sunday morning in January, 1994. The house was quiet, with no one else there. I was upstairs in my bedroom, lying on my right side, still sleeping. I know this because suddenly, with no warning, I entered into a startling, multidimensional awareness unlike anything I had ever experienced. I could see myself asleep on my bed, as if I were looking down at myself from the ceiling on the opposite side of the room. At the same time, I was aware of myself asleep in my body. I was startled and confused. What was all this? Looking back, I can see that even as my physical body slept, my subtle, spiritual awareness had just awakened.

And then, the next thing happened. It was as if this new consciousness itself took a slow, deep and deliberate in-breath as a means of gathering a powerful point of energy. I could see it and feel it, and I knew it was happening even as I was still asleep! Suddenly there was a great PULSE! of energy in the whole room, and my body was flooded with it. I responded to this in two ways. First, I felt extremely high – I was totally blissed out. Second, I said to myself, "It was worth living just to feel this!" "What!?" I began... but I was cut off. The force had gathered itself again as I lay there, still on my right side in bed, not yet physically awake. I anticipated another big pulse of energy, but instead, the energy formed itself into a column of opalescent blue light in the far corner of the room. At this point I felt a tremendous sense of excitement and fear. The column of light then snaked across the open space of my bedroom, came around behind me and lined up with my spine. Immediately my spine "opened" as if it had hinges and the column of opalescent blue light came into me – and my spine "closed" around it. Then I spoke aloud these words: "**Okay, Mike, come**

on in!" This woke me up fully. I sat up in bed feeling bewildered, as I looked around the room, then said to myself, "Who the hell is Mike?" I immediately got my answer. I heard these words in a still small voice at my right occiput. "Archangel Michael."

"Yeah, right!" I said. "I'm not even going to repeat that to myself!" But the most telling thing was that I went right back to sleep, feeling fully at ease with the whole experience. To my surprise, I spoke of my experience the next day with someone I trusted. I think I was checking to see if I was crazy. I spent the next six months trying to figure out what this all meant. About two weeks after my experience with Archangel Michael, I came across an advertisement in a new-age journal for the Conclave of Michael. When I read the ad I thought, "Wow! So many people have had an Archangel Michael experience like mine that they are going to have a meeting!?" I had to learn more. I immediately called the organizers, who were in Santa Fe, New Mexico. They faxed to me all the info on the event. That was when fax machines output a continuous sheet of paper, and the one I got on the Conclave of Michael was about thirty feet long. There I stood, scanning this long sheet of paper, looking for why I might attend the Conclave. Nothing got my attention, until I got about fifteen feet into it. There it was, a word that rocked me when I read it! ***Melchizedek***. Then another: ***Merkaba***. I did not know what these words meant. I had never heard them before. I was electrified!

The Conclave of Michael

I called to sign up for the Conclave of Michael right away. This event was held at the Banff Springs Hotel in Alberta, Canada, in March of 1994. As I was on the phone booking my room in Banff, I heard the words in the back of my head, "Stay nine nights." Because of this, I asked if I could get the conference rate for my stay before and after the event. They said yes, so I booked my room for nine nights. Then I started to research rental cars to get from the Calgary International Airport to the Banff Springs Hotel. Avis was offering a good deal on a Cadillac. It was white and it had 4500 km on the odometer. This trip included a numerology intensive. The number nine showed up everywhere; 4500 km on the odometer – numerologically a nine (when you add the digits). The altitude of Banff was 4500 feet, another nine. The room I ended up with was number 63 – another nine. The number nine showed up over and over again. The significance of the number nine in numerology is that it marks endings and beginnings. This trip was both an ending and a beginning for me.

At the Conclave of Michael I was drawn only to the work of Drunvalo Melchizedek, who soon became my first spiritual teacher. After Drunvalo gave his talk about the nature of this reality, entitled "A Love Story," I knew he was my next step, whatever he did. The next day I sought out Drunvalo's booth in the sales area set up for the conference. I found it, and a guy named Doug was manning the booth. Behind Doug, at the back of the booth, the wall was covered with several large crystals wrapped in wire. Doug and I made eye contact. As I began my question, "Do you have…," everything on the wall behind Doug crashed to the floor. I got the message. I had been about to ask for some kind of reading list to get me started; instead I asked for the info on when the next Flower of Life workshop was.

Drunvalo Melchizedek and The Merkaba

A few weeks later in Newburyport, Massachusetts, I attended my first Drunvalo training. It was only seventy miles from my house. Ninety days later I was at Drunvalo's teacher training, held in Austin Texas, in April of 1994. At this training I had several powerful experiences. The first took place while I was practicing the Merkaba meditation early one morning. I had gone to the workshop training room to do my meditation. As I sat in the blissful state of my fully activated Merkaba field once again, my consciousness suddenly shot out of the back of my heart chakra, traveled out and up and over my head in an arc, then flew back into me at my third eye area. When I crossed into what I expected to be the inside of me, I experienced shooting out into the entire cosmos. I experienced the entire reality within me. What a rush!

The energy of this training in Austin really stretched me. One evening, as I was getting ready to go for dinner, I had a very strange experience of bi-location. As I opened the door to my hotel room to go out, I saw myself in the form of dense energy standing at the door as if to come into the room. At the moment I acknowledged this energy form as me, we merged.

Later that night in the hot tub, I heard a couple of my classmates talking about some guy called Sai Baba in India. I remember thinking – "No way am I going to go get ripped off by some faker in India." But the seed had been planted. I was in India to see Sai Baba later that year for the first of many trips.

Tom Kenyon and the Hathors

A couple of months later, I connected with my next teacher, Tom Kenyon. I was standing in a parking lot in Sedona, Arizona, when Barbara Sheridan drove up with Tom Kenyon in the passenger seat. At the time, Barbara was an organizer for Drunvalo and others. The first thing I saw was Tom's very intense eyes: I could feel the power of his energy field from ten feet away. Barbara got out of the car and handed out flyers about something called a Hathor Workshop. I had no idea what that was. But I could feel the power of it, so I went.

At this workshop I connected with the power of sound, and at this workshop I got started. It happened like this. At the end of Tom Kenyon's first Hathor workshop, Tom did what I call a go-round, where everyone had an opportunity to speak of their experience during the workshop. I was about three-quarters of the way around the room, and when it was my turn to speak, I knew just what I would say. First, I had to say that I felt I knew Tom well, even though we had just met. While I did not know how this could be, I felt sure of it. Tom chuckled at this. Second, I had to say that I felt I understood what Tom was doing with sound, and while I did not know how this could be either, I felt sure of it. Tom laughed at this as well. Third, I had to make my commitment to this new/old understanding about sound in front of those gathered, who would be my witnesses. So, for the first time ever, I did about two minutes of toning in front of the group. This was a big deal for me. At the time I thought of myself as a "computer guy from Boston." Toning is not something I would have expected of me at all, never mind in front of other people. I learned much from Tom Kenyon in the coming years, but more on that later.

Chapter 2

Kevin Michael – A Brief Biography

"Truth is available only to those who have the courage to question whatever they have been taught."

-Anon

My Beginning

So, where did I come from? I was born in Boston in 1949 into a dysfunctional Boston Irish Catholic family. I was five years old when my father became ill. After having been a pilot for Pan American World Airways, my father developed kidney disease, went into the hospital, and it seemed years before he came out. Actually, he never did return. The man who came home was broken, angry and ill. He was also crazy and mean. Sometimes he was violent, as I learned over the coming years. My mother, always the picture of health, carried the ball for the whole family of eight, including six kids. She walked everywhere, or took the bus to get into the city to work. Karma's a bitch, and my childhood was likewise, no surprise there. It's a very common story, lots of violence, not enough love. I hated everything about it, with the exception of my mother; we were not a close or happy family. Everyone pulled themselves through one way or another. After twelve years of nuns as "teachers," I got out of high school with a scholarship to a little college in Maine. I did not thrive as a college student. The beer drinking was fun, but I had no real interest in the education. I left there and convinced myself that liberal arts was not the route for me to go. I then got myself accepted to Wentworth Institute of Technology and studied Aeronautical and Space Engineering. Still a disinterested student, I enjoyed the class if I liked the teacher, otherwise not. A course requirement at Wentworth was two drafting classes per week, however, I could not draw a straight line with a ruler! As a result, the teacher assigned me to the group who could not draw. What he gave us instead, were exercises in graphic isometrics. As a result, I very much enjoyed the mental process of figuring out what the multisided figures would look like when folded, or the other way around. After one semester I decided once again that this was not for me. This was during the Vietnam war, and I was subject to the Army draft. To avoid that, I joined the US Navy.

US Navy

After I enlisted in the Navy, I was given the usual battery of tests. I did well and was given more testing. Finally I was given a sheet of polygons to fold and another one of polygons to unfold, just like the exercises I did in drafting class. I completed the test. I did them in about a minute and got them all correct. Practice makes perfect! The enlistment officer was all excited and offered me the opportunity to go to the Naval Nuclear Power School in Bainbridge, Maryland. I said why not. I went, but I did not stay. I ended up stationed in Hawaii for three years at Subbase Pearl, working on the same submarines I would have gone to sea on, had I stayed in Nuclear Power School. I guess it was meant to be! I entered the U.S. Navy at age nineteen and got out just under four years later at age twenty-three with an early out of about two months, as was common at the time.

Marriage

I got married too early at the age of twenty four. My first daughter was born within the year. My second daughter was born two years later, to the day. In the aftermath of a very messy divorce and ten years of marriage, I began my personal inner work at about age thirty-five. The journey from there led me to a style of inner work developed by Fritz Pearls.

Digital Equipment Corp.

At the time my first child was on the way, I was looking for any job that would give me good benefits, (this was 1972 when good benefits could still be found). I did find one and began working for Digital Equipment Corporation, commonly known as DEC. I soon took over the company's logistic operation at Logan airport. After a couple of years I worked my way into a materials management job in manufacturing. I learned a great deal in a short time. It was a lot of fun working for DEC, when it was growing at the rate of 50 per cent per year. There was always lots of work to do, no time for bullshit. I made my way from manufacturing to field service logistics, then on to an engineering support role and new product development. After getting my first management position, I found I was in trouble. I did not know how to sit in the conference room and "say the right thing"; honesty not required. It scared me to be in an environment that I had no capacity for. So, I made a lateral move into information services, where my specific company knowledge was valuable. I was in a position to learn many new technical skills and I liked this job more than any other job I'd had. As a systems analyst, I could use my existing knowledge while developing new technical skills. At least that was my plan.

Ill Health

The Harmonic Convergence occurred in August of 1987. At that time, I thought astrology was nonsense; therefore, the Harmonic Convergence was a non-event to me. Little did I know! Within a year my health went completely to hell. Chronic fatigue syndrome and environmental illness became my day to day reality. In 1989, after two years of attempting to cope with electromagnetic hypersensitivity at work, I collapsed in my office. The fluorescent lights and the computer screens (cathode ray type) made me very ill. I walked out that day and never returned.

Jin Shin Jyutsu

In 1990, I began to receive acupuncture as a way to hopefully help myself heal my health problems. After a couple of years of acupuncture, I discovered Jin Shin Jyutsu, a no-needles form of meridian work from Japan. This continued for a couple of years, until I decided to study the technique for myself. I did so, and after taking the class three times, I became a certified practitioner. Jin Shin Jyutsu helped me greatly to recover my life force, and get it moving correctly again. I still practice on myself nearly every day. It was after the first six months of daily practice on myself and with others that I had my experience with Archangel Michael. I am sure that the practice of Jin Shin readied me to receive Archangel Michael. In Jin Shin, the practitioner focuses on the ONE Pulse. For me, Archangel Michael came as the ONE Pulse.

Hypnotherapy School

Years later I attended hypnotherapy school. Gil Boyne, one of my teachers who was also the senior mentor of the school, taught us the process he had developed. It was very similar to the one I used. While I had learned my technique from students of Fritz Pearls; Gil had worked with Pearls directly at the Esalen Institute in California decades before. I felt at home with Gil Boyne. His style appealed to me, especially his generosity and compassion. In his eighties, Gil was usually very direct, you could tell where he stood.

I will share more of my personal journey of healing and remembering WHO I AM as we go forward in this book. For now, let me introduce you to The Bridgers. The Bridgers are members of ascended humanity who are empowered to serve as your agents. What the Bridgers do is carry your request to Source on your behalf. I will let them speak for themselves.

Chapter 3
A Word From The Bridgers

"The quieter you become,
the more you can hear."

-Ram Das

"We are the Bridgers, and we will help you. You are not alone in this task of personal healing. Know that we will help you each and every moment of your lives. You need only accept our help. How to do this? Ask. Here is how to ask. We are led by the Master Jesus, and he has empowered us to simply remove those things that cause you so much pain. You must understand what this means. Each form of suffering has, at its root, some cause. **You do NOT need to know the cause. You simply allow Source to remove the cause**. We do so on your behalf by taking your request to Source, and Source removes the cause. Eventually, some of you will be able to do this directly, but for now we are your willing servants; it is our service to you and to Source, and we provide this foolproof link on your behalf. When you ask us to remove a cause, it will be removed. The ultimate goal of all of this is your personal freedom to make your own connection to Source in a pure fashion. There is no longer anything stopping you from becoming free of inner pain and suffering. The Master said, 'Ask, and you shall receive.' We are here to help you to ask more effectively and efficiently. We are your servants. We are your brothers and sisters who have gone before you. We know your pain. We know your loneliness. We know your lonely love. We wish to restore Divine Love in your daily lives. This is the purpose of this book. We have a mission to serve your well-being. We have a mission to restore your Divine Love. We have a mission to serve humanity in this way. It is our great pleasure to do so. In this book, we will lay out the means to do so. We will give you 'chapter and verse.' We will help you with each step. You are in good company now. You are ready to live. You are ready to be one with Source in your daily awareness. You are ready to hold a brighter Light here on Earth. The time of seemingly pointless suffering is over. The time of Love and Life is here. The time of peace and kindness is imminent. Become ready; heal your histories now. Heal your hearts now. Do as we guide you and accept God's Love fully today. Do it Now! Say this: 'In the name of the Master Jesus, I accept God into my heart NOW.' Through this book we will teach simple techniques for removal of negative patterns from the subconscious mind. There are no situations that will not yield to this work. There are no people unable to benefit. All are able to benefit from this work for the simple reason that they do not have the **doership** of this work; all they do is ask for help from us (the Bridgers), and we relay the request in a pure and focused way to Source, Who is the Doer. The doership of this technique belongs to God. If you go and ask the butcher to slice some meat for you, are you the doer? No, you are the asker, the requester. With the butcher it is only you and the butcher who are involved. With this removal technique, we (the Bridgers) are the go-between for you (the asker) and God/Source (the doer). Know that you can only benefit from the process. If you ask to remove the cause of your addiction, and it fails to completely go, have you failed? NO. You have perhaps asked with less clarity than needed, but the asking will start a process of deepening that will lead you to more clarity in the matter. Perhaps you will wish to work with an experienced practitioner to help you focus. Why do you suffer from addiction? Is it because you are a loser or a bad person? No! We will guide your requests to us, which we then relay to Source. Ask and you shall receive. Ask well. Be informed of what you are asking. Be ready to do the steps required in all sincerity and openness. Be ready to receive Grace from Source as a result of asking through us. We are here to help. We are here to make it simple for you. This book contains some guidelines and suggestions on how to proceed in different areas of life. It is good that you have this roadmap."

I have been working with this technique and its' precursors for the last twenty years. The Eureka! Moment for me was when I realized that it is most effective to ask that the NEED (subconscious, karmic patterns) be removed. The "need" is the cause of the issue. This need will be subconscious content, karmic in nature, and may come from one or more other lives. While I have learned to dig deep and find the reasons why these patterns exist, in order to dismantle them one step at a time; that process has always been costly in terms of time and money. With this process, we simply go to Source and ask that the need for the issue be removed; the result is that we stop creating it and it is suddenly gone. This is a much more practical answer to the real-life need for personal growth and change NOW. I have written this book as the next step in getting this self-help technology out into the world. I have been given the task of bringing this method to the many. In so doing, I have been asked to see to it that initiations and trainings be offered. To this end, I have now produced this book. The training schedule will be posted at www.kevinmichael.net

---

The Dialogue between Harry and Swami that follows in chapter 4 will introduce the Bridging technique. Make the choice now to experience the removals for yourself as you read them. You can say to yourself, "I choose to receive the benefits of these removals as I read them." You can even write in your own name if you wish. A blank space has been provided for you to write in your own name to help you benefit most fully.

Chapter 4
Harry Meets Swami

***"Fear is the cheapest room in the house.
I would like to see you living in better
conditions."***

-Hafiz

"Remove your fear of god!" Harry heard these words as he sat in meditation after asking for help on his spiritual path. Harry's reaction was immediate. Joy mixed with fear. Elation that he had just received inner guidance, and fear that he did not know what it all meant. Getting direct inner guidance was exciting but unknown to him.

He felt a bit intimidated by all this. Harry had never before heard such a direct Inner Voice; never before had he been given such direct instructions on the inner plane. "How do I do that?" Harry asked himself.

The answer came in as a booming inner voice: **"Yield!"** The word shook him to his roots. "You must surrender to the Source of the one reality," Harry heard, feeling a bit bewildered.

With the question formed in his mind, Harry felt a bit sly as he asked "How, exactly?"

"I will show you if you ask," the Voice said. Harry considered this for a moment, and soon felt fear.

"How do I know I can trust this?" Harry asked himself.

"You must have faith," said the voice. "Trust and allow," the voice continued.

Still feeling intimidated by all this, Harry felt himself surrender to the fear, and shut down inside. His previously cocky attitude gone, he no longer felt sly. He no longer felt in control. "I don't know how to do this," he said to himself. "Who or what am I supposed to trust here?"

"I AM" said the Voice.

"What the hell does that mean?" Harry wondered.

"The Divine Presence within you," the voice answered.

When Harry heard this in his mind, something clicked inside his heart. He felt a deep sense of knowing that what he had just heard was Truth. As Harry absorbed the realization he was having about himself, he also felt doubt. "How can this be? I can feel it, but I can't believe it!" And then, "Yeah, right," Harry said to himself, "The Divine Presence within me. Like I could believe it."

Harry decided to challenge the Voice and clear this up. "You expect me to believe the Divine Presence is within me?" Harry asked out loud.

"Don't get a big head over it." said the Voice in reply. "The One Being which exists pervades every person, place and thing in existence. There is only One, There is no 'other,'" the Voice continued. "You are a direct expression of this One Divine Being," the Voice finished.

"So, what, you're telling me that I'm some kind of special thing here?" Harry challenged.

"No," said the Voice. "You are just part of the whole."

"Okay, then, I can go with that," Harry said.

"The fact that you are a direct expression of God does not make you special," said the Voice. "It is simply the Truth, the same Truth for everyone. It's only human ego that makes a claim to be special. You are a drop in the ocean of consciousness, no more, no less. The only question is this: Are you ready to acknowledge your SELF?"

"How do I do that?" asked Harry.

"You can do this in a number of ways," the Voice went on. "An easy way to do this is to simply picture yourself as a drop of water in the ocean, feeling safe and secure in your natural environment, then realize the one ocean is made up of trillions of drops like you."

Harry considered this for a moment. "So you're telling me to give up my individuality?"

"No," said the Voice. "I'm inviting you to see the Truth. Your individual expression as part of the One Being will continue as long as you find it useful. There is no threat possible to Who You Are, only to who you think you are. This is the fundamental issue – misidentification. You think you are a lowly human being, so you are. This misunderstanding is the common burden of the common man. I have come to help you get beyond these limiting beliefs, this limited self-talk."

"How?" asked Harry, as he began to feel curious about all of this.

"If you can accept my help," said the Voice, "I will guide you through a process that will remove your negative beliefs.

"You can do that?" Harry felt this was a pretty big claim to make.

"YOU can do that, Harry, with the right help," answered the Voice. "The goal of this inner work is greater awareness of 'Who You Are,' and the result of this inner work is more freedom! Let 'More Freedom!' be your rallying cry, as well as your personal goal. More freedom to know the Truth of who you are; more freedom to live life as a happy and loving person; more freedom to choose your direction in life. More Freedom to Live!" Then the Voice asked, "Is this something you would like to have?"

"Okay," said Harry. "There are some things I have to get clear first. Like for starters, who are you? Here I am having a conversation in my head with a dude, and I don't even know who it is or if I'm nuts."

"I am your Bridger, if you'll have me," the voice replied.

"What does that mean?" Harry challenged.

"Bridgers are beings in spirit who are available to help beings in physical bodies to become more free."

"What shall I call you?" asked Harry.

"You can call me anything you like," said the Voice. "I have had many names. My role is simply to help you go forward on your path."

Harry thought for a moment, then had an idea. "I think I'll call you Swami!" Harry declared aloud. "It's easy to remember, and I like the sound of it."

"Very well," Harry heard in his head, "you can call me Swami."

"What do we do now?" asked Harry.

"If you are ready," Swami answered, "we can begin."

The way Harry heard Swami's voice in his mind was a little strange. It felt like a knowing he somehow was sure of; at the same time, he felt the words, as much as heard them, as Swami spoke to him on the inner plane. Harry smiled to himself at the thought that by some great luck he had made a solid connection with his spiritual guide.

“Not luck.” Harry heard the words on the inner plane. “You have arrived here after much toil; you have earned this Grace,” said Swami.

“I’m ready to get started,” Harry declared, now very curious to learn more.

“One of the most basic and biggest problems human beings have is misidentification.” Swami remained silent as Harry thought about this.

“What do you mean by that?” asked Harry.

“Misidentification means you think you are something you are not,” Swami replied.

“But I am a person, what else?” Harry thought to himself.

“You think you are your body; this is a mistake,” Swami replied.

“So you heard my thoughts?” asked Harry.

“Always,” replied Swami.

“Oh, okay.” Harry felt invaded. “Are you going to listen to every thought I have?” asked Harry.

"Yes," Swami continued. "If you will have my help, I will stay in constant contact with you."

"What about my privacy?" Harry asked.

"If you wish, you can set a specific time for our work together," Swami replied.

"I think I'd like to do that," said Harry. "That way I will feel more comfortable with all of this."

"Very well, it will be as you wish," Swami answered. "You can begin a session of work with me simply by saying you wish to begin. I am always available to you."

"Can we begin a session now?" Harry asked. "I am curious to know what it will be like.

"Yes, Let us begin now," said Swami.

More about "Bridging"

"Bridging" is the term I use to describe the work we will do together," said Swami.

"Why do you call it 'Bridging'?" asked Harry.

"We call it 'Bridging' because the technique depends entirely on the involvement of a 'Bridger'; I am the Bridger working with you. There are many others. Long ago, the Source of All That Is saw the need to provide help to those who wished to return home to Him sooner. Because Third Density is too dense for most human consciousness to reach beyond, most people needed help. While most have a concept of God, only some have a direct relationship with Him. Source of All That Is chose to provide help to those who need it, and Bridging was established. Those of us who serve as Bridgers are go-betweens. We have ascended to a level of consciousness that includes direct communication with Source. We are here to serve in that capacity. **This is a form of prayer**, with a Bridger as your go-between. On your own, you can say the words in a small human voice; with help from a Bridger, your tiny human voice comes through loud and clear in the mind and heart of Source. Additionally, Bridgers can advise and assist with your spiritual development. This is not a new idea. In the Christian world, Jesus has served as the Bridger to very many people. In Asia, Buddha has done the same. Most cultures have saints to whom the people make their petitions. It is time for all people to know: you are free to have our help without conditions. No religious affiliation is required. No religious affiliations or beliefs would prevent you from having our help if you ask. The Bridgers are members of ascended humanity who have put themselves in service to not-yet-ascended humanity. **Our goal is your freedom from suffering. We serve all who ask for our help. All you must do is ask.**"

Chapter 5
Removal of My Need to Feel I am My Body

"Your identification with the body is the impediment to your spiritual growth."

Anon

Swami spoke to Harry: "And so to begin, we will work with the idea you have of yourself that you are your body." Swami continued, "In fact, you are the Divine Presence, expressed as Harry. Your animal body is occupied by spirit, and this spirit is Who You Are in fact. You are the consciousness, the spirit that occupies your physical body. Notice that it is common for people to refer to 'my body' or 'your body.' Who is the one who speaks of that body? Who is it that speaks of their body as a thing that belongs to them? Human bodies are vehicles for Spirit. When you say the word 'I,' do you refer to the body or the being in the body? A human being is spirit in a body, God in a body. You must *Realize* that you are Spirit in a body in order to get the full benefit of the information."

"And how do I do that?" Harry wondered out loud.

"Do not be concerned," replied Swami; "we will remove the obstacle to your realization, and then you will understand."

"Okay," said Harry, "let's do it!" Harry felt a combination of doubt and curiosity; he was now determined to find out if this stuff worked.

Swami continued, "We begin by doing a removal of **Your *Need* to feel 'I am my body.'**

"Sounds weird to me, but go ahead," said Harry.

"The form we will use will be consistent from one piece of work to another," Swami explained. "And so, are you ready to proceed with the removal?"

Harry decided to just go ahead with it, even though he could have asked more questions. "Let's do it," he said. Suddenly there was a shift in the energy Harry was feeling. He felt embraced by light.

"We begin," said Swami at the same moment. **"This is the removal of my *need* to feel I am my**

body," said Swami. **"This is for Harry, ____________________ and we begin now."**

Immediately, Harry felt a slight jolt of energy move through his body. Then he glimpsed a vision where he was the circus master, announcing the animals from the center of the ring. There were the elephants, the horses, and a big black bear. They all moved in a circle under the Big Top. Riding on the horse was a pair of chimpanzees. "Oh my God!" thought Harry, as he saw his face in one of the chimps. "I think I get it!" Harry felt his own Presence very strongly as he saw his own face in the chimp. "I am not my body!" Harry declared. "I am definitely not that monkey!"

"Well done," Swami said. "You have seen for yourself what you are not."

Harry felt quite different after this experience. "I feel like someone else," Harry said to Swami.

"You have had the experience of being the Observer," replied Swami. "As the Observer, you are free to see from any perspective; you are not bound by your body or its physical location. You can observe from your inner vision as well as your outer vision."

"This will take a little while to digest," Harry thought to himself. "Something is definitely happening," he mused.

"How was that for you?" asked Swami.

"Amazing," Harry replied. "I saw that who I am is the observer of my life as well as the person involved in my life. Imagine! All that from a circus monkey!"

"Very good," said Swami. "Let's go on."

"Okay," said Harry, wondering what could possibly happen next.

"This is the removal of my *habit* of feeling that I am my body," said Swami. **"This is for Harry, ____________________ and we begin now."**

Again, Harry felt a light jolt of energy run through him as he had a vision of himself being tortured in a dungeon. Harry was startled. "What the hell is this?" he said out loud.

"Do not be afraid, Harry," said Swami. "Your vision was a past-life memory, and one you are better off being done with. Remember," Swami continued, "we are REMOVING these things from you. In this case, your misidentification as a physical body was greatly reinforced by intense physical pain and fear. You have just now seen more of why you had the very strong habit of identification as the body – physical pain. When you are in enough pain long enough, you begin to identify with it. Remember, you have seen all this as it was being removed from your subconscious mind. Be calm; feel safe. You are fully protected by the Divine Presence as you do this purification work, and," Swami concluded, "you are doing very well."

Harry sat there feeling strangely alive, and a bit confused.

"Your identity is shifting from a 'less than' human to a Self-Aware Being. You are doing very well," Swami continued. "Are you ready for the next step?"

"I guess so," Harry answered. Harry was feeling a little disoriented, but also very curious about what could be next.

"Last, we will remove your denial that you feel you are your body. Before we do this, I will recap what we have done so far," Swami continued. "First, we removed your '**need**' to feel you were your body. Notice that we did not say what that need was. We only asked that it be removed. Second, we removed your '**habit'** of feeling you were your body. Habits result from repeating something over and over. Your need existed long enough to create a habit. So we removed it. Last, we will take out your '**denial'** that you feel you are your body. Why? After having a need for a long time that you did not understand; you generated a habit that you had no real control over. You then did the only thing left to do; you denied that the problem existed. This of course has no impact on the problem other than to hold it in place. In order to deny it we must hold it away from ourselves, which is to say we hold on tight to the thing denied. So, the removal of the denial is an important step to complete the removal of the pattern."

Harry felt full to the brim with all this, so he simply said, "Okay, let's do it."

"Very well," replied Swami. **"This is the removal of my *denial* that I feel I am my body. This is for Harry, ____________________ and we begin now."** Swami completed the statement.

Again, Harry felt nothing at first. Then he remembered to surrender to the prayer. Suddenly, Harry saw a high wall, made of bricks, come tumbling down. The rubble was swept away, leaving a clear view of young Harry in a shallow pit. Up on the edge of the pit was a beautiful rainbow-colored Being of Light. Somehow, Harry understood this was

Harry himself, who and what he really was. As Harry acknowledged this to himself, the shallow pit rose to the level of the surrounding earth. Suddenly he was face to face with this beautiful Being of Light. Something in Harry's heart then told him that he was this Being of Light. Harry felt awed by this. "How can this be?" Harry thought to himself. "I'm just a …." Harry's thoughts faded as he felt Swami's presence.

"This is Who You Are," said Swami. "This is the Divine Presence which is you."

Chapter 6

Harry Merges With His Higher Self

"This connection to the Higher Self is probably the most important thing that could happen in your life."

-Drunvalo Melchizedek

"Are you ready to merge with your higher self? asked Swami.

Harry sat there with an incredulous look on his face. "Well, I'm, I'm… not sure," he said, feeling both excited and intimidated at the same time. "What if it does not work for me?" asked Harry.

Harry could feel Swami's benevolence as He said, "Do not be troubled, Harry. Your Divine Presence knows when it is time to show up. You can trust this."

“But what must I do?” asked Harry, both hoping to be able to do it and wondering what it all meant.

“Say yes to it,” answered Swami.

“That’s all?” asked Harry.

“Say yes to it with all your heart,” continued Swami. This is your Divine Presence, for whom you have been waiting.”

Harry could feel the simple Truth that this beautiful Being of Light was actually his essence. “How do I say yes?” asked Harry, feeling excited to be so close to such a good thing in his life.

“In your inner vision, take a step towards your Presence,” Swami guided, “and he will take a step towards you. Go ahead, take the step,” urged Swami.

Harry did as he was told. He took one step toward his Being of Light, and his Being of Light took one step toward Harry.

“Now, take another step,” urged Swami.

Again, Harry did as Swami suggested. Harry took another step, and this time his Being of Light took another step at exactly the same moment. Harry now felt so close to his Being of Light that he could hardly tell where his edge was. It felt to Harry that they had begun to merge. Harry heard the words "Join with me." Then Harry heard himself say "Yes" out loud. At this same moment his Being of Light merged with him. It all happened so fast that he did not have time to react. One moment he was plain old Harry; the next moment he was one with his Being of Light. "What just happened?" Harry asked aloud.

"You have just merged with your Divine Presence," came the reply from Swami.

"What does this mean?" Harry asked, feeling happy and a bit disoriented at the same time.

"You will discover what this means as you live your life," Swami answered. "It is basically a major turning point on your spiritual path. You could say that this is the real beginning of your spiritual path. With this connection established, you have the means to grow more quickly and more deliberately than ever before. Do you remember you have at times felt that life was a long, lonely road, never feeling sure where you were going?"

"Yes," said Harry.

Swami continued. “Now you have your Divine Essence active within you. Congratulations! You have entered the surest track for your spiritual growth. Much will come to you now that could not come before; your integration with your Divine Presence guarantees it,” Swami finished.

“But what does it really mean?” asked Harry.

“It is your way home,” replied Swami. “It is your guarantee of success on your path; it is Grace that you have received in abundance.”

“But why did it happen?” asked Harry. “I don’t know how I got here,” said Harry, still feeling incredulous.

“Be still,” said Swami, and know Who You Are. “Be still, and feel gratitude for this attainment.”

“Why do you call it an attainment?” asked Harry.

“This event, this blessing of receiving your Higher Self into your awareness, surrounding your physical shell, is something you have long sought,” explained Swami. “On the inner planes of consciousness, your commitment has long been recognized by those who serve the Light; there is much joy in heaven at your accomplishment. You are not alone.”

"What do I do now?" asked Harry.

"Take a nap," Swami instructed, "or go for a walk, and relax in full acceptance of your gift received and your attainment that made you eligible for it."

And now, we'll give Harry a little time to himself and return to the story of my spiritual journey.

Chapter 7

Egypt 1994

"And You?
When will you begin
your long journey into yourself?"

-Rumi

After I connected with Drunvalo and the Merkaba, Egypt popped up on my radar. Drunvalo told a story about his visit to the Great Pyramid and I was intrigued. In addition to this, at my first workshop with Tom Kenyon, Tom introduced us to the Hathors; beings on the subtle planes of this reality. The Hathors are strongly associated with Egypt. As a result, Egypt had my attention. I did not know if or when I would make the trip, but it did feel inevitable that I would go there.

I was with some friends in Sedona, when I heard about an Egypt trip being organized out of Santa Fe,

New Mexico. It was billed as the 12:12 Egypt Trip, scheduled for December of 1994. Preliminary information suggested it would be a large group, a couple of hundred people. There was a presentation about this trip scheduled at the La Fonda Hotel in Santa Fe, New Mexico, the next day. Although I thought it unlikely that I would join such a large group, I felt drawn to Egypt, so I decided to go and listen to the presentation and see what I would learn. A friend joined me for the trip to Santa Fe, and the companionship was welcome.

On the way across the desert, just east of Gallup, New Mexico, I had a very simple vision. The vision was of a fan-shaped wall sconce with the color red at the top and regular light from a plain bulb on the bottom. The light was on, with the fixture in the middle of a big, otherwise empty wall. I had no idea what it was. At the time I was not accustomed to having visions, so I just filed it under "I wonder what that is." The drive across the desert went well, and we arrived In Santa Fe in plenty of time for the presentation. The presentation was at 7 pm at the La Fonda. After getting some supper, we arrived fifteen minutes early for the presentation. As I walked through the door into the La Fonda function room, I looked up across the room and there it was – the fan-shaped wall sconce with the small red light at the top in the big, blank wall, which was otherwise empty. Actually there were two of them, left and right of center, where the stage was set up. When I saw them I froze for a second, because I felt that this confirmed the Egypt trip for me, and it showed me that this was probably the group I would go with. The size of the group no longer mattered to me. I had gotten my confirmation.

December 1994

On the way to Egypt, I connected through Zurich, Switzerland. The sun was just coming up as we flew above the clouds, about a half hour to go before landing. I looked out the window and saw the majestic mountain range of the Alps soaring above the clouds as we approached Switzerland. What a glorious sight! To me, this was the first major event of this trip. I felt so uplifted by the natural beauty and grandeur of this mountain range! This marked the real beginning of my journey to Egypt. Then the seat belt sign came on and we started to get ready to land. The Zurich connection went smoothly and we were soon airborne again, heading to Cairo.

The arrival area was a bit of a shock. When I found my bag at the luggage area, I saw that the locks had been cut off. Not only mine, but others as well. This felt odd, but it was nothing compared to the young, armed soldiers standing guard all over the place. I decided the best thing to do was get out of the terminal and find my ground transport as quickly as I could.

The transfer to the Mena House Hotel in Cairo went smoothly, and I was glad for a quiet room with a bed. The Mena House is a unique hotel, with its own rich and colorful history. It is surrounded by forty acres of verdant green gardens, and I could see the Great Pyramid of Giza from the grounds.

The next day there was a meeting set up at the Mena House to get the whole group together for the first gathering. Some of our group members were staying in another hotel nearby. This meeting sounded like a routine and necessary review of our in-country logistics, which it was. However, there was also a big surprise for all of us.

The first thing we heard from the trip's organizers was that they did not have the money to deliver the land package to all of us. What a welcome to Egypt! The organizers made their confession by explaining that they had used a lot of the trip deposit money for a bigger advertising budget in order to get more people to come on the trip! As a result, they were short thousands of dollars. We had about ten people, out of over 200, who had scraped together the airfare to Egypt. They were the last people to sign up (they were also the youngest in our group). As of that moment, they would not even have a place to stay that night, unless something else happened. Well, something else *did* happen.

After we were done being shocked and angry at our betrayal by the organizers, a consensus quickly formed. We took up a collection on the spot, and put together the nearly $15,000 needed to cover the land package for these ten people. An excellent group cohesion formed as a result. Nothing was going to stop us! We were on a mission! I'm not sure we really understood what that was at that moment, but it felt great! With the budget repaired, we made our way to our hotel rooms to prepare for dinner and a good night's rest.

The Isis Temple

The barges were a comfortable means of transport on the Nile River. Our barges arrived at their berths near the Temple of Isis at Philae. There was a sound and light show at the temple that evening. I'm not much of a tourist, so I did not think I would go to the show. At the last minute, though, I left my berth and quickly made my way to the small motor launch that took us to the temple. I never saw the sound and light show.

As the motor launch approached the temple dock, the energy moving through me, took me over. Although I had never been here before, something in me knew what was up. I had one foot in the air at the moment the prow of the launch tapped the side of the landing. I jumped onto the dock, ran up the steps and my feet took me where they wanted me to go. It was as if I had no say in the matter.

It was nighttime, and the artificial light was low as I quickly made my way to the temple entrance. I passed into the outer courtyard, intrigued by the spot but unable to stop. I quickly continued, as if I knew where I was going, through to the inner courtyard. At the far side of the inner courtyard, I came to a rope barrier, which I knocked down as I just kept going further into the temple. Now it was dark, but my feet kept moving me forward. I continued all the way back to the inner chamber where the granite altar stood. It was about four feet high and a solid block of stone.

As I came abreast of the right side of the altar, my left hand shot out and touched the altar in a probing manner. "Damn!" I heard myself say. "Where are they?!"

Whatever part of me was running the show at that moment, my personality was not part of it. As I heard myself say "Where are they?" I could also feel that this other part of me was expecting something to be on top of the altar, but it was not there. I did not have any time to think about this, because my feet just kept moving with a purpose. I completed a U-turn around the back of the altar and headed back out. As I returned to the area with some light, I remember looking up and seeing the beams that held up the temple roof. The symbol of the winged solar disk and two cobras was carved into each of the beams. Even moving fast in the low light, I was still very aware of the imagery.

I popped back into the inner courtyard, where I felt myself stop moving suddenly. Some strange energy had gotten my attention and I had to stop. Looking around, I saw strange carvings at the tops of the columns that surrounded the inner courtyard. I was captured by the energy that filled the night. When I looked up, I saw what looked like a low cloud deck, just about six feet above my head. As I gazed up at the “cloud deck,” out of the corner of my eye, I saw a woman standing at the other side of the courtyard. She stood just in front of what is known as the Mammisi or birth house. Suddenly my attention was drawn forcibly and fully back to the space above me. Through the “cloud deck” above my head, a large ankh, almost as big as me, was held forth by a hand that extended below the “clouds.” The hand then placed the ankh directly into me. At the moment this was done, the vision changed to the Talons of Horus. This felt to me like a command, insisting “Don’t mess this up!” The woman at the side of the courtyard was now gone, I never learned who she was.

The Great Sphinx

Our large group would arrive on buses, then disperse in the general area of a temple complex, where we would all go exploring as we wished. At Karnak, I wandered over to a subsidiary temple room that felt very powerful to me. The outer wall of the room was missing and you could see and hear the traffic jam on the street outside. Even with this distracting background, I was still captivated by the space. I sat in meditation for a while until a temple guide showed up and began to explain what the room was. It had been the actual inner sanctum of the temple. He explained that just in the next room, candidates for initiation would be tested. Seated in a power position, such as on a throne, candidates would be told that they were to serve as judges on that day. Offenders would be brought before them, and after hearing their offenses and their pleas, these candidates would have to decide the offenders' punishment. After having done so, they would be welcomed into the fabulously rich environment of the greater Karnak Temple. What they did not know was that they had failed the test. The test was to see if they were willing to be judge and jury for other people. If they agreed and did so, they failed the test. If they refused to do so, they would be welcomed into the inner sanctum, the room I was sitting in, where they would receive their initiation, having passed the test of the Temple.

There were many other tombs and temples that we visited on this part of the trip, but the best was saved for last. We flew back into Cairo, where we returned to the Mena House. I recall feeling that it was time for a small group to form for the purpose of getting inside the Great Pyramid. Accordingly, I walked to the outdoor café on the grounds of the hotel and sat at a large table. As I sat alone sipping my tea, I waited to see who would join me. I knew my group of like-minded conspirators would gather at this table. Within the hour we had gathered there, and we agreed to meet at dusk and head to the Great Pyramid.

After being challenged by a couple of rifle-toting guards and paying them some baksheesh (bribes, an ever-present activity in Egypt), we were left alone at the feet of the Great Sphinx. One of our group had a need to study an inscription etched in stone, located on the chest between the paws. For me this was no problem, I did not know what to do next anyway. However, we did not stay in that spot long, as the flying insects drove us out. We went off in different directions to explore the whole of the Great Sphinx as each of us wished. I walked along the base of the great structure and was surprised to see that the surface was composed of many large bricks of white stone, as if it had been recently repaired. It seemed that repairs were indeed under way, as there was a ladder placed against the side of the Sphinx. I took the opportunity to climb up. It brought me to the back of the Sphinx, where I walked up and down looking for something interesting. Finding nothing on the back of the Sphinx, but the white stone it was made of, I climbed back down. I continued to explore along the perimeter of the monument. Eventually I came to the back of the Sphinx's right paw where I found a small opening. It was in the back of the right shoulder, just above my head. I had found a flashlight on one of the busses a few days before and had it with me. Standing on a brick of white stone, I aimed the beam of light into the opening; which was now about the same height as my eyes. The space inside was large enough to consume the beam completely. I could see nothing. I had heard it said that there was an opening to an inner temple behind the right paw of the sphinx. Maybe so.

The Great Pyramid

Finished at the Sphinx, our group of seven headed for the entrance to the Great Pyramid for our meeting with Amun. We had met Amun earlier that day, at his nearby shop; where he offered to help us get into the Great Pyramid. Amun was an hour late for our appointment, so all we could do was wait. When he finally arrived, our so called 'help' to get past the guards, ended up with us paying more baksheesh to both Amun *and* the guard.

The guard just disappeared, for a few minutes, and we were in. We entered the Great Pyramid well before midnight. I was amazed at the internal structure of the building. The inside appeared narrow and rough-hewn at first, but as we went further into the pyramid, I began to see some of the complexity of the construction. There was no time to dwell on architecture, however as we quickly found the tunnel to the left, that descended far down to the subterranean chamber that contains the Pit. The tunnel ran straight and continuously down at an angle of twenty-six degrees. The tunnel was about four feet high, three and a half feet wide and 300 feet long. When first built, there was no light inside. Fortunately for us, electric lights had been strung all along the passageway, and they had been switched on for us. We quickly made our way down the tunnel. For me, it was mostly a matter of keeping my head down and sliding on my hands and feet. Once we were all in the chamber that contains the pit, each of us did as we were drawn to do. Then we took some meditation time together. After that, I went exploring around the chamber. There is a smaller tunnel cut into the bedrock at the far wall, opposite the entrance tunnel. One of my teachers had explained that this was a place of instant manifestation. That is to say, if you were to crawl into this small tunnel (about two feet square) and then allowed yourself to go into fear of any kind, the thing you feared would manifest immediately. According to my teacher, many people have died in that tunnel. At the time I was there, it was closed off by a heavy steel gate and padlock, so, I could not get into the tunnel. That was probably all for the best, as I doubt I had enough awareness, at that time, to survive it. When we were all done exploring the Subterranean chamber, we decided to do some toning together. I stood at the edge of the pit with another member of my group who was very much into sacred sound (toning). She and I began, and the rest of the group joined in. We had been at it for a couple of minutes, when suddenly the lights went completely out! I felt that the darkness added to the power of what we were doing and experiencing. In any case, we had no control over the lights, so we just continued toning. For me, toning goes along naturally with planting a column of light at the place where I am making the sound. The thought of the column comes by itself, and then I intend it, and it happens. When the column of light formed, it was gigantic! It was the most powerful column of Light I had ever experienced! I assumed it was enhanced by the Great Pyramid itself. Then the next thing happened! The column, which had been spinning clockwise suddenly reversed itself and was now spinning counterclockwise. I was stunned! Then I remembered the Merkaba, (a body of light formed from the energies of Spirit) and the fact that it spins counterclockwise. I had to wonder, was I impacting the pyramid or was the pyramid impacting me? I think the latter. Shortly after this, the lights came back on. By then we were all very ready to leave the pit, so we all quickly climbed back up the 300-foot-long tunnel before the lights went out again.

At the top, we were near the inside of the front entrance to the Great Pyramid once again. Most of the group headed for the Queen's chamber. I felt drawn to the King's Chamber, and headed there by myself. I found the Grand Gallery, the route up to the King's Chamber, and started to climb. As each step up the gallery took me closer to the entrance to the King's Chamber, I felt the power of the place more and more.

Finally, I arrived at the top of the Grand Gallery and the entrance to the King's Chamber. At this point, the passage into the chamber was so low, I had to get on my knees and crawl in; sort of an imposed state of humility, you could say. Then I was in. The room thrummed with its own energy. I took it in. I walked around, sliding my hands on the walls, looking for whatever I might find. I became a bit short of breath as the energy of the room increased the flow of life force through my body. So, I decided to sit against the wall to take it all in. As I sat there, I began to sing a chant I had learned from Tom Kenyon, “El Ka Leem Om”. Tom referred to the chant as the Hathor Chant, or a way to call in the Hathors, (higher dimensional beings of ancient Egypt). I sang the chant at the top of my lungs for a couple of hours. The biggest thing I noticed was that the King’s Chamber itself seemed to return to me more energy than I was putting out with my chant. I became more and more energized as I chanted. Suddenly, my attention was drawn to the sarcophagus, which sat in the correct spot according to my teacher. It was located in a “Golden Mean” relationship to the chamber, which was itself a Golden Mean-shaped room. The term “Golden Mean” refers to the ratio of the length and width of the room. Also called the Divine Ratio, this geometry is considered optimal for consciousness, as it results in a frequency that is the same as the human heart chakra, or Love.

Suddenly I stopped chanting. I went over to the sarcophagus and climbed in. I lay down in the stone box and made myself as small as I could so I could fit inside it. It was a tight fit, like lying down in a small bathtub. Knees up, I squirmed my head this way and that, intending to position my third eye in the correct spot to catch the beam of energy said to be generated by the geometry of the King's Chamber. At first I had no luck – then suddenly, I found the spot. Instantly, I experienced my awareness expanding. It seemed as though my consciousness (the spiritual being that I actually am) shot out of my third eye, and I instantly became one with the whole cosmos. My body lay there scrunched into the sarcophagus in the King's Chamber as my consciousness became one with all that is! An awesome experience! It did not really stop, but simply faded as it became familiar. As I continued to take it in, I heard another sound. Someone else was in the King's Chamber! I raised my head up over the edge of the sarcophagus to see what was going on. As I did so, an Asian woman turned and saw me lying there in the coffin. Startled, she sucked in a breath, speechless. I realized it must be daytime now, and the pyramid was open again for visitors. I had been in the Great Pyramid all night! I climbed out of the coffin, and the Asian woman looked relieved to see just a guy standing there, looking at her. I wished her well and headed for the exit. As I passed by her, she smiled a smile of relief. I got to the top of the Grand Gallery on the way out. High as a kite from my experience in the King's Chamber, I wrapped my elbows over the railings on either side, then swung my legs up and hooked my feet over both railings and slid all the way down the Grand Gallery to the bottom. I made my way to the door of the Great Pyramid, dodging the tourists coming in. Once I reached the outside, the daylight was intense. I walked all the way back to the Mena House hotel in an attempt to get grounded. It was no use. Back home in Massachusetts, it took me about six weeks to integrate the energy of this experience. That's how long it was before I could even sort through the mail!

And now, let's return to the next part of the Dialogue with Harry and Swami.

Chapter 8

Removal of My Need to Lack Faith

"To the one who has faith,
no explanation is necessary.
To one without faith,
no explanation is possible."

-St. Thomas Aquinas

"What is the way to home?" Harry was unsure if he heard this or thought it as he came out of meditation early one morning. **"I Am,"** boomed a voice in his head. Harry felt a bit confused by both the question – which had arrived fully formed out of nowhere – and the equally unexpected answer that filled his awareness. Unsure what to do with all of this, Harry turned to his inner guide, whom he now knew as Swami, to ask him for help. "Swami, what does this stuff mean?" asked Harry.

"You were given the question to ask that will help you make more progress on your spiritual path," answered Swami.

"What about that other thing I just heard – **I Am**?" asked Harry.

"**I Am** refers to your Inner Divinity," said Swami. "Now that you have joined with your 'I Am Presence,' you will find it urging you ever onward, guiding your inner work with strong *suggestions*," explained Swami. "The question and the answer came from the same Source. Your Higher Self is now guiding your inner process. This is normal."

"So, what do I do with this stuff?" asked Harry, unsure of himself.

"Surrender to it," Swami continued. "Accept it as inner guidance and work with it."

"How?" asked Harry.

"The question and the answer came from the same Source," repeated Swami. "They both came from your Inner Divinity. So you can see," Swami continued, "the **I Am** is both your vehicle to get home to God as well as your immediate goal. It is as if your Higher Self has reached down into the dense human plane of consciousness, to make contact with you in order to pull you up to Him. So, the goal is unity with your Divine Self, and the route to this unity is to take His hand. Every day. And do your best to respond to His inner guidance. Every day."

"It sounds like a lot of work," said Harry.

"You may find it so at times," said Swami. "However, the alternative is to stay asleep and risk falling even further asleep. Your path has been made clear. Your Divinity has contacted you. It is time."

"Okay, I guess you're right," replied Harry. "What do we do next?"

"I'm glad you asked," answered Swami. I suggest we do a piece of work on the subject of faith."

"Why faith?" Harry asked.

"Because you need faith to overcome doubt," answered Swami.

"But I am feeling good about all this right now, so why…" Harry's thought faded away. He was starting to get the idea that he was better off listening than arguing. "Okay, I will do as you suggest," said Harry. "I think you know what you're doing." Harry felt a deepening within himself as he accepted the idea of surrender on this point.

"You are wise to surrender," Harry heard in his head. "Letting go of your personal will in this matter speeds the process," continued Swami.

"I felt more relaxed about all of it once I chose to surrender," Harry replied.

"A wise choice," Swami confirmed. "Are you ready to continue?"

"Yes let's go on," said Harry. "I am ready to see what I can learn by working this 'faith' topic."

"Okay," said Swami. "We begin. **This is the removal of my *need* to lack Faith,"** Swami intoned. **"This is for Harry, ____________________ and we begin now."**

Immediately, Harry felt a big expansion in his crown chakra; then he felt a light pressure at the top of his head. Suddenly the pressure increased, pushed through his skull and flooded his head, then his whole body. "Whoa!" Harry thought to himself. "This feels awesome!" Harry sat in the bliss of this energy, which now moved throughout his body. "What is this?!" Harry asked excitedly.

"You are experiencing the direct connection with Source," said Swami. "Congratulations! It seldom comes this soon after beginning your inner work. You are blessed."

"What next? asked Harry.

"Now we remove your habit of lack of faith," answered Swami.

"We still need to do that?" asked Harry.

"Yes," replied Swami. While we have removed your need to lack faith, you still have the habit created by the long-term behavior."

"But I would have thought the last step did it all," Harry objected.

"You think you are the expert already?" teased Swami.

"Okay, okay, I get the message," said Harry. "Let's keep going."

"Good! Now we can continue," said Swami. **"This is the removal of my *habit* of lack of Faith,"** Swami stated. **"This is for Harry, ____________________ and we begin now."**

Harry was sitting quietly as he heard Swami declare the intention. Suddenly, as before, he felt a little jolt of energy up his spine. As the jolt of energy flooded his head, he saw the anger and contempt he felt for organized religion. It flashed through his awareness all at once. What he saw was not new to him, but he realized it all differently. He realized how his religious background, confusing and spiritually corrupt as it was, had destroyed his faith. Harry suddenly felt in his heart that faith is a good thing. He realized that he had thrown it out along with what to him was the corrupt religious crap he had grown up with. But that was a mistake. "I threw out the baby with the bath water," Harry realized. Just then, with his inner vision, Harry saw himself reach out and pick up his infant of faith, then hold it lovingly to himself.

"Good job," Harry heard Swami say. "You have given yourself another great gift. You have reclaimed your innocence."

Harry felt full of emotion, mostly love and gratitude. "I feel more safe now," Harry said to no one in particular. It was more his personal realization that he spoke out loud, just to anchor the feeling. "Swami," said Harry, "I feel more safe now, and I feel

I can do much more with this work that you have brought me."

"I am very pleased for you once again," said Swami. "You are obviously ready for this. Let us go on," Swami continued. "Next we will remove your denial that you lack faith."

"It seems redundant," Harry commented.

"You have had to deny your lack of faith all of your life," said Swami. "And in denying this lack, you have held it in place."

"Okay, I think I get it," said Harry.

"Trust the process," replied Swami. "It is only your small self, your ego, that is opposed to change. Human egos like to be in control. The problem is, the human ego is tied very much to survival, and it does not like change. Progress on the path of self-realization requires trust. You must trust in your Greater Self to bring you to Him."

'Okay, okay, I get it," Harry surrendered. "Let's go on."

"Yes, let us continue," said Swami. **"This is the removal of my *denial* that I lack Faith. This is for Harry, ____________________ and we begin now."**

At first Harry felt nothing, then suddenly he had the vision of a brick wall collapsing. "This is... starting to feel familiar," Harry thought, as his vision continued to unfold. There he was in the shallow pit, about age ten, and feeling very lost. Harry remembered that this was around the time he started to think for himself. It was also the time when he had begun to object to the religious teachings he had been given.

Harry remembered how he used to feel good about God. As he began to see things he did not like, his faith failed. He dropped the whole thing, mostly out of sadness that it all appeared false. He now saw that human failings and corruption were just that – human. The Divinity itself is not about any of that. "Okay!" Harry thought to himself. "I'm doing the right thing here." Then Harry spoke out loud: "Swami, thank you for helping me get my faith back."

"You are most welcome," replied Swami. "I am pleased to be working with you."

Harry felt his stomach growl. "I'd better get something to eat," he thought. As he started to get up out of his chair, he noticed a change in the energy he had been feeling. Harry quickly sat back down and waited pensively for the good feeling to return.

“Do not be concerned,” said Swami. “It is normal to feel different when in session: the energy is higher. When you break from a session, the energy naturally drops back down to normal waking consciousness. This energy is at a lower frequency. Go and have your lunch now,” urged Swami. “When it is time to resume our work, you can be sure the energy will be there, even if you do not notice it at first.”

“Why would I not notice it?” asked Harry, a little worried he could miss out.

“You will find at first, that you transition gradually from your normal waking state, as you turn your attention to your inner world. Likewise, there is a shift from your inner awareness state, suitable for doing this work, to your outer awareness state, suitable for eating lunch.”

“On that thought, I’m hungry!”, Harry stopped for lunch.

As Harry sat enjoying his food, he reflected on his morning’s experience. Harry noticed he felt different than ever before. He felt light somehow, and quietly excited that he had arrived at this new place in himself. Then Harry wondered to himself, “Can I use this technique for other issues? It seems to me I could. I think I'll ask Swami when I get the chance."

Suddenly Harry dropped into a light trance, and at the same time he heard Swami say, "Yes, you can use this technique for many issues in your life. Harry smiled at the fact that the answer had come so quickly; this was unexpected, and he felt grateful for it. "This is nice," thought Harry. "I'm lucky to have this going on." Harry finished his lunch and went for a walk. It was a beautiful day, with a soft, cool breeze under a clear blue sky. "I wonder how long I will be doing this," thought Harry. "It seems to me there are very many topics in my life that I could use this technique for."

Suddenly Harry thought, "What does He call this method? I forget what he told me."

"Bridging," Harry heard in his head.

"Hmmm, I wonder what that means," Harry mused. "I will have to ask Swami about it again, at our next session."

And now it is time to tell you the story of my first trip to Puttaparthi, India to visit the ashram of Sathya Sai Baba.

Chapter 9

Sai Baba in Puttaparthi, India

"Life is either a daring adventure - or nothing at all."

-Helen Keller

January, 1995

I made my first trip to visit Sai Baba in January of 1995. As this was my first trip to India, I went with a group. A fellow traveler found a new hotel in the village, and we booked rooms there. At the time, Puttaparthi, India was a little town at the end of a long road, about four hours by cab from the airport in Bangalore. The cab ride was amazing. It seemed the cab driver thought we were more interested in speed than anything else. I shared a cab with a woman from the group, who was also traveling to see Sai Baba. We rode in a nondescript-looking white four-door sedan. I sat in the front and she sat in the back.

The cab driver was a young Indian man who seemed anxious to please. However, his idea of giving good service included passing every other vehicle on the road in a mad dash for our destination. I was frightened again and again as our driver passed the vehicles in front of us on the road, one apparent near miss after the other. This included passing large, colorful long-haul busses and trucks. These vehicles were painted in a riot of colors depicting their protective deity, often with mantras painted in bold colors over the top of the windshield. The sight of an oncoming vehicle in the opposite lane never slowed him down; he would always be passing another vehicle or getting ready to do so. Now and then he would have to squeeze back into his lane because he could not find a hole through which to pass. All of this was accompanied by endless blaring of the horn. All the vehicles involved were blasting their horns all the time. It appeared that constant use of the horn was a regular part of driving in India; I later learned that it was. I was not very comfortable with this style of driving, but this was my first time in a cab in India and what did I know? Meanwhile my companion in the back seat was white as a sheet with fear. Eventually it became apparent that this crazy cab ride had to stop. I told the driver to pull over. He looked at me strangely and kept going, his horn blaring, his foot on the gas. I told him again and gestured that we pull over to the side of the road. Again, he looked confused, pointing to the road ahead of him. Finally I started yelling at him directly to pull over and stop the car. He looked at me like I was crazy and kept going in the same manner. He would not listen, it seemed. I kept up the loud demand that he pull over, pointing to the woman in the back seat trying to get him to see her fear. Finally he pulled over, more from his confusion over what this crazy American man wanted, rather than any understanding of the situation, or so it seemed. His English was a bit thin, but finally I got him to understand that we wanted a SLOW ride to Puttaparthi. He looked mortified as we drove off again. I believe he felt he was giving us the best service because of his speed and maneuvering, and he did not understand why we did not appreciate it. Many cab rides later, I learned that what I had experienced on this first cab ride was somewhat normal cab driving in India.

My first visit to Sai Baba's ashram, known as Preshanti Nilayam (abode of peace), happened the next day. I had gotten up about 4 am to attend morning darshan with Sai Baba. The routine in Puttaparthi included morning darshan, with the queue (waiting line) beginning as early as 4 am. Then afternoon darshan with the queue beginning after lunch at about 1 pm. The term 'darshan' refers to the sight or presence of the holy man. Walking along the street from my hotel to the ashram gate at that early hour always felt a bit eerie. Light came from small fluorescent bulbs here and there in front of peoples' homes or shops. The occasional streetlight cast a dim island of yellow light, leaving most of the street in shadow. The air was cool at that early hour, and all the local people who were at the tea stall wore shawls, sometimes wrapped around their heads to keep warm. They were accustomed to 100-degree weather during the day, so a cool seventy degrees called for more clothing.

Entering the Ashram

As I approached the ashram gate, called the Ganesh Gate, I was assaulted by beggars. I managed to avoid them and entered through the gate. Once inside, with no more beggars to deal with, I stopped to take in the scene. Directly in front of me was a large shrine to Ganesha, the remover of obstacles. Many people were cracking coconuts at the foot of the shrine, offering the milk and prayers to Ganesha as a part of their morning puja (spiritual

ritual). Ganesha is the wisdom aspect of the Divine. The idea is to appeal to the wisdom aspect of God to have your path cleared for the day. Ganesha removes all obstacles, you just have to ask. I did not know any of this at the time.

As I stood there taking in the scene in the half-light, a strange energy began to engulf me. Suddenly I felt as if I'd been picked up by the collar of my shirt and flung up into the sky. There I experienced myself tumbling through a cosmic-sized Ganesha for a full minute. I could no longer see the people milling about. The sound of the pujas ceased as I tumbled through space inside this cosmic body of Ganesha. What a rush!

When I came in for a landing, the pujas were still going on and the number of Indian people milling about had increased. I remembered where I was and why I was there, and began to look around to see where to go next. I saw a small procession of men coming towards me. They sang in the most beautiful, powerful voices, full of earnest focus and devotion. It seemed as if they knew where they were going, so I joined them. I did not know it but I had just joined the daily morning procession, on their way to the darshan hall to sing the first prayers of the day. I stood with them at the small Krishna shrine on the left side of the Mandir (temple) until they completed their service. When they dispersed, I followed them out of the darshan hall. On the way out of the hall, I encountered a man who looked official, so I asked him where I should go next. He smiled, and pointed out the gate and down the slight hill to the left.

Following his directions, I walked down the concrete paved way, it was like a giant sidewalk or small road. I passed between the darshan hall on my left and one big, four-story concrete building which was a set of dwellings, kind of like an ashram condo on my right. This building was at the edge of the ashram property and shielded the darshan hall from the endless noise and activity out on the street. There, during the day, everything was packed in close: the buildings, the people, the cars, the trucks, the donkeys, the bullock carts, everything and everyone. But it was early morning, still blessedly quiet, and I was in Sai Baba's ashram for the first time!

Darshan with Sai Baba

Just ahead I saw a group of guys sitting on the ground in the sand. Here was the queue for the darshan hall. There was a seva dal (service attendant/security man) nearby, and he pointed to a spot for me to sit. I sat down on the ground, the last guy in the last line. Shortly afterward, they called my line to go into the darshan hall; all the others had already entered. It was my first time, and I was comfortable knowing nothing. Wherever the next seva dal pointed, I went. The line made its way to the security scan and I passed through without difficulty. The seva dals were all over the place, and a questioning look to one of them got me the guidance of a hand gesture or a pointed finger and I knew just where to go. I was guided by one seva dal, then the next, and I ended up in an area at the front of the men's side, which I came to know as the 'piano top'. The shape of the area resembled the flat top of a grand piano. The location of the 'piano top' was to the left of center of the Mandir and just in front of it. The 'keyboard' ran just along the main darshan walkway that Sai Baba used every day as He walked through the crowd of men sitting on the floor. The walkway turned right at the left hand end of the 'keyboard', then continued up along the long side of the 'piano top'. Just inside what would be the end curve of the 'piano top' was one of the pillars that held up the vast roof. Here, the walkway turned right and went around the pillar. At the far end of the 'piano top', it then turned down in a graceful long arc, which was physically represented by a two-inch-high curb of concrete in the correct curved shape. The short side of the 'piano top' was defined by a line of tile from the low end of the graceful curve, back to the right hand side of the 'keyboard'.

Each day, Sai Baba would walk along the 'keyboard', turn right along the long side, turn right around the pillar at the end curve and come slowly down along the long, graceful curve. This location was the usual end of Baba's darshan walk each time. I had seen Him take exactly this path each and every day.

My First Letter to Sai Baba

After several darshans with Sai Baba, I began to feel very agitated. I did not understand why. Finally I noticed other men handing Sai Baba letters, and I decided to write a letter of my own. That night, back in my room, I sat at the desk and began writing. Very quickly I realized that what I was writing was bullshit and I had to do better. Time after time I crumpled up the page and threw it over my shoulder. Frustrated that I had not written anything real, I got up and fumed around the room. What did I need to say? I decided I needed to tell Him the truth, no matter what!

With this in mind, I began writing again; this time telling Him exactly how I felt! I wrote about how hard I found my life to be; how painful and sad, full of loss and loneliness. How I felt betrayed, helpless, hopeless and alone. I wrote of my feeling abandoned by God and how angry I was at him for creating this horrible world, with all of its' pointless suffering. I told Him how I felt like a prisoner behind bars for life. I wrote of my frustration with God, and whatever the hell He was up to. Finally, I wrote about surrender. Again, I let Him know how I felt! The last line of my first letter to Sai Baba was – "I give up, you son of a bitch!"

I felt amazed and concerned at what I had just written. Even though I had not given Sai Baba the letter yet, I was sure I would do so. The time was already 3 am, so there was no point in going to bed. Sleeping was out of the question anyway. I decided to take a hot shower and get ready for darshan. I made my way to the queues and sat down at the end of the line that was forming on the museum hill walkway. This was a sort of line before the lines, where you waited for the lines to officially form. I ended up back on the long curve of the "piano top," the same place I had been directed to every day I had been in the darshan hall up to that point. I would have a long wait to give Sai Baba my letter. Finally Baba came out and made His way across the hall to the men's side. Getting closer to where I was with every step, Baba did His usual thing and stopped to greet a man in the front row. He would chat him up a little, then materialize vibhuti for him and pour the sacred ash into the man's hand. Sometimes, Baba would indicate that it was okay to share the vibhuti, and other times He would say "Only for you". I have seen this manifestation of sacred ash directly from Sai Baba's hand many times. One time His hand was only about ten inches away from my face as He created vibhuti for a devotee near me. With His fingers tented, forming a kind of channel for the vibhuti, the ash would simply pour forth from the space just in front of the center of His palm. It looked to me that the ash simply came into being in the space He defined with His tented fingers, always pouring out into someone else's hand.

Baba continued His slow walk through the hall, greeting many as He walked by. My anticipation began to build as Sai Baba approached the top curve that went around the Pillar at the end curve of the "piano top." His next few steps would see Him begin His slow walk along the long curve to where I was seated in the front row. Just as he made the turn around the pillar, He did something different. Instead of walking down along the graceful curve, He began to head straight for the Mandir steps nearby. "Oh, no!" I felt panic. "What if He doesn't take my letter?" I suddenly realized I had no idea what I would do. I had just assumed He would take my letter. I was completely committed. In my mind I began to plead with Sai Baba. "Baba, you've got to take my letter! Please! I need you to take my letter! Please take my letter!"

I was on fire with the intention that Sai Baba take my letter. Yet with each slow step He took, He moved a little further away from me. I felt desperate. I pleaded within once more. "Baba, I really need you to take my letter. Otherwise, what am I going to do if you don't take it?" I was not prepared to be rejected by Sai Baba. Just then I was reduced to real humility by the realization that Sai Baba might not take my letter. I kept my eyes on Him with a burning pleading that He stop moving away from me and come and take my letter. Within me, this was about whether or not He accepted me. I truly felt that Sai Baba had guided me, even pushed me, to write this nasty letter to Him. I did not know what I would do if He did not accept my letter.

Suddenly, Sai Baba stopped moving and turned toward me. He looked straight at me as I held out the letter, and in a few steps He was near me. Not waiting until He got closer, I reached out a little more, holding the letter up to Him. In one move, He stepped in closer and yanked the letter out of my hand. Good job!, He seemed to say. He had accepted my letter! He had accepted me! Even with all the vile acrimony in my letter He had taken it! I was saved! He accepted me as I was after all!

And now It's time to return to Harry and Swami and see what they are up to.

Chapter 10

Removal of My Need to Stay Small

"Argue for your limitations and sure enough they're yours."

-Richard Bach

After an enjoyable lunch and a brisk walk outdoors, Harry felt ready to do some more work. As Harry relaxed into his green La-Z-Boy, his office felt warm and inviting. "I'll just stretch out for a little after lunch nap," he thought. Harry pulled up the lever on his chair to the full reclining position. Feet up, head back and feeling fully supported, Harry quickly dozed off. Harry was fully at ease, when suddenly a light came on. The light was a greenish gold color. He could smell a sweet scent of honeysuckle flowers, but none were in the room or at the window. All he could see was the greenish gold color.

"Are you ready?" Harry heard a calm voice in his mind.

"Yes," Harry heard himself say, all the while not knowing what was going on, or even where he was.

"You are dreaming," said the Voice. "Your dreams will help you more and more now."

"Oh," said Harry to himself as he struggled to roll over, only to find he was still half asleep in his easy chair. Harry decided to stay in the chair and sleep a little more.

"Your life is your own," said the Voice. "You must decide how to live it."

Groggily Harry spoke. "Yes, it is mine, it is mine, it is up to me." Suddenly awake, Harry had the realization of what his dream state had been telling him. "What I do with my life is for me to choose," Harry said aloud. Feeling a little confused at first as he came out of sleep, Harry rubbed his face with both palms to wake himself up. "Damn right!" declared Harry, now fully awake. "What I do with my life is for me to choose." Harry reached for the red water glass that he kept by his chair and took a drink. "Damn straight! What I do with my life is for me to choose." Harry felt firm in his declaration that it was his choice what to do with his life, yet he had a vague sense of foreboding. It was as if there was something he did not yet understand.

"All rested now?" Harry heard the familiar voice in his head.

"Well, sort of," replied Harry. "But I do have a question."

"Your question is most welcome!" replied Swami. Harry felt good and safe talking with Swami in his head.

"I just awoke from this crazy dream where I woke up declaring that what I do with my life is up to me, and only up to me," continued Harry. "Then, as I came fully awake, I said 'Damn right! It's up to me!'" Harry paused a full minute as he thought it through. "It's as if that all makes sense to me, but I'm not actually doing it."

"Good insight," replied Swami. "This tells you what to work on next."

"It does?" exclaimed Harry, bewildered.

"Yes," answered Swami. "Your dream was telling you something about being true to your Self, Who You Really Are," Swami continued. "What I speak of is different from any conventional view of a person. 'Who You Really Are' is God in human form."

"How can that be?!" cried Harry. "I'm just a guy who likes sports and works for a living. How is that God?"

"When you speak of your mundane life," Swami replied, "you invoke your mundane awareness. There is a much greater life available to you. But come, let us get back to work, for this is the very thing we are working to change."

"It is?" asked Harry, surprised.

"Yes, we are working to remove your limitation and the obstacles on your path to a far richer life," Swami answered. "A productive, peaceful life with happiness and contentment. Let's go on now. Your dream suggests a good line of approach. From your dream you concluded that you are in fact in charge of your life, and yet you do not *feel* in charge of your life."

"True enough," said Harry. "I don't see what else is available to me."

"No, you don't," said Swami. "Your beliefs about yourself act as filters that block out all but your familiar limited view."

"So what do we do?" Harry asked.

"**We remove your *need* to stay small**," answered Swami.

"Okay, you're the boss," said Harry. "I am glad to have your help."

"Let us begin," said Swami.

Harry settled into his chair and got comfortable. "Okay, I'm ready," said Harry.

"Sit still," Swami instructed, "and take a slow easy breath, then blow it all out." Harry did as he was directed. "Again," said Swami. As Harry repeated the deep, easy breath, he noticed he felt more relaxed. "One more time," said Swami. After his third deep breath, Harry felt centered and relaxed.

"I think I'm ready," said Harry.

"You are," confirmed Swami. **"This is the removal of my *need* to stay small,"** intoned Swami. **"This is for Harry, ____________________ and we begin now."**

Harry felt a slight shift inside himself, as if a full-size, three dimensional overlay of himself had just been pulled out of him. Harry felt a little jolt of energy in his body, then noticed he was bathed in a beam of white light. It felt so good that Harry did not want to move, lest he break the spell.

"The beam of light you are feeling is the purification beam. It comes from Source, and it is guided by you and me," explained Swami. The Bridgers have been given this gift and the duty to use it. You might not always notice it, but it is always there for you.

"Thank you," said Harry with deep sincerity. "I see I'm being given great help. I am grateful."

"Ask and you shall receive," quoted Swami. "There is much powerful help available to you from the subtle planes of existence."

"What do you mean by subtle plane?" asked Harry.

Swami answered, "The subtle planes of this reality are where you will find most of the beings which exist in this Creation. The subtle planes of reality vibrate at a higher rate than the third dimension, so you cannot see it with your physical eyes."

Harry suddenly recalled the feeling he had just had, while they were doing the removal. "I felt as if a whole body overlay of me had been pulled out of me, during the last removal; was that a different vibration like the ones you were talking about?"

"What you felt was a different vibration," answered Swami. "But it was a *lower* vibration. The overlay you noticed as it was removed consisted of various fears and beliefs about yourself, which were the main reasons for the removal. They were a *lower* vibration, and they had held you down," Swami explained. "Congratulations on dumping them! Are you ready to go on?"

"Yes, let's do it!" Harry replied.

"Very well," said Swami. "We will go on. **This is the removal of my *habit* of staying small,"** said Swami. **"This is for Harry, ____________________ and we begin now."**

At the moment Swami completed the phrase "begin now," Harry saw a clear picture of himself as a child sitting on his father's lap as his dad was speaking to his uncle Jim. "All you have to do is keep your head down, and you'll be all right," said Harry's dad to uncle Jim. "Just stay under the radar and blend in," his dad continued. As Harry witnessed this vision/memory, he realized he had taken in every word as if it had been spoken just to him. And, he had accepted it as true for himself. And then Harry saw clearly how he had lived his life "staying off the radar" and "blending in." Harry was thunderstruck at this realization.

"You seem a bit agitated," said Swami. "What did you see?" he asked.

"I saw that I have chosen to stay small," Harry answered. "It's what I learned from my father, and he wasn't even speaking to me at the time; but I heard his words and I made them my own right there on his lap as he was speaking to my uncle Jim. I was five years old."

"Good find!" said Swami, urging him on. "You are doing a great job of allowing yourself to see the roots of your beliefs."

"Okay, what's next? I want this one out of me NOW!" declared Harry.

"Let us continue," Swami went on. "Please take a deep, easy breath and become centered once again."

Harry did so, and as he did, he felt enriched by it. "Ready," said Harry.

Swami spoke: **"This is the removal of my *denial* that I need to stay small. This is for Harry ____________________ and we begin now."**

In his mind's eye, Harry saw a wall tumble down, clearing his view of the scene beyond it. There in a shallow pit he saw before him an image of himself at about age five. He was sitting on the ground, playing with his toy truck. Up on the edge of the pit there was another toy truck. It was beautiful. He really wanted to go and play with it. But, when he felt the impulse to stand up and reach for it, he felt a hopeless feeling at the same time and he could not stand. In the scene, little Harry just went back to playing with his firetruck, longing to play with the other toy truck but knowing in his heart he would never reach for it.

Swami spoke to Harry very kindly and asked, "Are you ready to change this?"

"I hope so," said Harry.

"Okay," said Swami, "let's get little Harry some help. Stay with your vision and let us change it. First, you need a strong ally to help you at age five. Who would you like to have with you?" Swami asked.

"I think Jesus would be good. I knew about Him when I was five," answered Harry.

"Okay, now stay in the scene in your inner vision," Swami instructed, "and we will remake it."

"Okay," said Harry.

Swami proceeded to guide the events in Harry's vision. "Now, Harry, you see a beautiful face with very loving eyes."

"Yes, I see them," said Harry.

Swami continued, "This is Jesus, who has come to be with you and help you."

"Oh, yeah...." Harry relaxed greatly in the presence of Jesus' Love.

"Now that Jesus is here to help you, what happens next?" prompted Swami.

"I ask Him to get the other truck for me," Harry replied.

"I will help, you will do it." Harry felt this more than he heard it.

"How?" Harry asked Jesus.

"We will give you the ability to choose," said Jesus.

"What does that mean," thought Harry.

"I will help you, you are not alone," said Jesus. "When you think of reaching up to the new truck, what do you feel?" asked Jesus.

"Scared," said Harry.

"Okay," said Jesus. "Put the feeling of being scared in a big bubble, right in front of you."

"A bubble?" questioned Harry.

"Just like a big soap bubble," Jesus answered. "Go ahead and put your fear in the bubble."

"Okay," said Harry, "It's in there."

"Good," said Jesus. "Now ask the fear why it is here. Go on and just talk to it like it is a person, and ask it why it's here."

Harry put his attention on the imagined bubble with the fear in it. "Why are you here?" asked Harry.

"To protect you," Harry heard immediately in his head.

Harry felt a bit annoyed. "To protect me from what?" Harry demanded to know.

"Yourself." Harry heard the reply in his head. "To protect you from yourself, and to keep you from taking a chance," said the fear in the bubble.

Suddenly Harry saw it. The fear he felt at taking a chance in life came from what he had heard his father say to his uncle Jim. "Keep your head down and you'll be all right." Harry felt liberated, no longer forced to "keep his head down," no longer forced by his own fear to stay small, no longer fearful of reaching for what he wanted in life. In his vision, the shallow pit rose up level with the surrounding ground. The new toy truck was right there in front of him. Harry leaned forward and took hold of the new toy truck. At that moment, as he sat in his easy chair, the adult Harry felt a jolt of energy move through him, and he knew at that moment that the fear was gone. He had overcome the fear – and now he had new choices available to him.

"Well done," said Swami. "You have removed a major limitation from yourself."

"And to think it was all because of something I overheard at age five!" declared Harry.

"And now you see clearly," Swami concluded, "how a well-meaning statement from your dad to your uncle Jim became a life sentence for you from age five onward. The good news is that you have removed it."

And now, let's return to my personal journey in India.

Chapter 11
The Dalai Lama

"Love is the absence of judgement"

-H.H. the Dalai Lama

<u>February, 1996</u>

I was on my second trip to visit Sai Baba in southern India. Just after darshan one morning, I went to a little restaurant called the Tibetan on Chitravathi Road. It was a regular haunt of mine because the people were friendly and the food was good. Tibetan food is not normally spicy, so I liked it very much. Just a few steps from the main gate of the ashram, the simple, quiet dining room was a nice break from the crowds at darshan and all the hubbub out on the street.

As I enjoyed my meal of vegetable Thenthuk soup and momos, I overheard a woman speaking very excitedly about this place in north India she called upper Dharamsala, where the Dalai Lama lives. As she spoke, my curiosity grew, so I decided to look into it further. I had just experienced the most powerful darshan I had ever had with Sai Baba, and I felt complete for that time with Him.

I had shaken hands with the Dalai Lama in Chicago a few months earlier. Looking back, I see that my connecting with His Holiness there in Chicago was the beginning of my visit to see him again in India. After a visit to a travel agent, I decided to go to Dharamsala. I felt it would be a good use of my time. I had one more week scheduled for my trip, and then I planned to return to Santa Fe, New Mexico, my home at the time. I had been invited to make a presentation at a large conference near Glorieta, a part of Santa Fe. This would have been the beginning of my public work, or so I thought at the time. It did not turn out that way.

The Tibetan community surrounding The Dalai Lama in northern India is located in a place called McLeod Ganj, (elevation 6831 ft.) approximately 2051 feet above Dharamsala (elevation 4780 ft). Dharamsala is located in the Kangra Valley, in the shadow of the Dhauladhar Mountains, in Himachal Pradesh, northern India.

I flew from Bangalore to Delhi, arriving at a late hour. I had no plan to stay in Delhi, so I needed to find a cab. After I paid more baksheesh, (only they don't call it that in India), a cab and driver appeared and I was on my way. It was a newer cab, red in color, with a very tired driver. I later learned he had been on duty for twenty-four hours already, but he had accepted the fare to Dharamsala, a further twelve-hour drive. Well, I was going, and that was all there was to it. He was the guy who showed up to take me, so that was that. It was after midnight by the time we were on our way. Twelve hours on the road ahead of me, and a sleepy driver to help keep awake. I chatted him up about anything I could think of as we drove away from Delhi. He seemed to settle in okay once we were out of the city and on the main road to Ambala. After Ambala, the road got smaller and was poorly maintained. This forced my driver to go slower, and that was okay with me. We passed through Chandigarh, Rupnagar, and on through Anandpur. Finally the sun came up, and both my driver and I became more alert. This was good, because the road had become more winding and hilly, so the driving was more demanding. After another stop for tea and a bite to eat, we continued on our way. Soon we were in the foothills of the

Dhauladhar Mountain range. We were now close to our destination.

No Reservations

As we drove through the outskirts of Dharamsala, my driver had an accident. It was just a fender bender, the result of my driver's exhaustion and the usual chaotic traffic in and around any populated area of India. When he dropped me off in Dharamsala, I gave him a large tip to help with the fender repairs that he would have to pay for. I paused long enough on my journey to eat a good meal, and found another cab, this time a local one. The driver knew his way around, and soon had me in McLeod Ganj. I had no reservations, so I told the driver to take me to the very best hotel in town.

The very best hotel in McLeod Ganj is the Chonor House. Chonor House is conveniently located close to the Dalai Lama's Home, overlooking His Holiness the Dalai Lama's Buddha temple. It was built by Norbulingka Institute as part of its endeavor to preserve and promote Tibetan culture.

It was the right move. My reason for going to the best place was to get the best service, and I needed help. It worked out well for me. I entered the small lobby of Chonor House and was greeted by an alert and attentive Indian man named Ravi (the name Ravi refers to the rising Sun). I told him my story, including the fact that I had no reservations anywhere. Could he help me? Ravi advised me that he could give me a room for that night only, and that he would see if he could find me another place in the morning.

I felt relief as Ravi handed me the key to my room. The Chonor House is a very lovely place with a very good feel to it. I felt lucky as I walked to my room. When I entered my room, I found it to be very cold. I looked around for a switch to turn on the heat and found nothing. I looked all around the room to see how it was heated and found nothing. I looked into the well-appointed bathroom and found a small space heater, not plugged in. Oh well, when in Rome… I decided I needed the heat the most in the bathroom, so I could shower more comfortably in the morning. Accordingly, I set it up and closed the bathroom door. I still had to deal with the fact that the room was cold, so I bundled myself up in a couple of blankets and sat in one of the big easy chairs and went into meditation. There were two easy chairs placed at ninety degrees to one another, a placement to facilitate conversation. Very soon I felt warm as I dropped into a deep meditative state.

The next thing that happened was a big surprise! Suddenly, the Dalai Lama appeared in spirit in the other easy chair and greeted me. “Welcome, I am so happy you have come!” I heard in my mind. “Let me introduce you to...” I then saw another figure in the room, this time a standing profile of a man, about five foot eight with a pot belly. I felt a distinct feeling, a quality of a strong Spiritual Light, held by this figure. Shortly afterwards, the visions faded. I wondered who this guy could be, that the Dalai Lama took the trouble to introduce him to me. Maybe a monk? I just didn’t know.

By the time I had finished breakfast, Ravi had arranged another room for me at another hotel. It was directly up the hill above the Chonor House and connected by what was almost a road. The road ran up the hill at a very steep angle and was not much more than a jumble of boulders. It was difficult to walk on and a car would never make it. The hotel porter was undaunted. A young Tibetan man, he put his arms through the looped handles of my wheeled duffel bag, carrying it like a backpack. He picked up my other small bag and held it in front of him, then marched up the hill as if there was nothing to it! As I began my climb up to my next hotel, he marched past me, going quickly up the hill with his heavy load. Just as I got close to the top of the hill, he came back down and passed me, letting me know my bags were already at reception. I thanked him and gave him a good tip.

I checked into my new hotel, the Hotel Bagsu. It was perched at the top of a hill, overlooking a vast area of sky. The hill was very steep, as it was actually the side of the mountain, Looking straight out you could feel the sky and the white eagles flying everywhere you looked! The eagles were the biggest I have ever seen. Their coloring was the opposite of what I have seen in Alaska or northern California. They had white bodies with dark coloring along the back of the wings. Oh! How they soared! Many hawks could be seen as well, and some birds I could not identify. I checked in to my room for a stay of about a week, or so I thought.

Joe

Then I met Joe. I was walking along the Potala Road when I saw a man who fit my vision from the night before. I recognized him by his profile and energy. As I came closer, he turned and greeted me.

Joe was very outgoing, and he enjoyed other people very much. He would stop and greet anyone he saw on the street. As a result, he quickly made friends with many people. As we got to know one another, I learned why Joe was visiting McLeod Ganj. Joe had gone to Sydney, Australia, from his home in Los Angeles, in order to attend the Kalachakra Initiation with the Dalai Lama. The Kalachakra initiation is one major purpose of the Dalai Lama's monastery. There in Sydney, Joe met a monk who asked him if he would come to McLeod Ganj and allow him to be his teacher. The monk who made this invitation worked directly with the Dalai Lama, and had also served as his teacher! In the end, Joe could not pass this up. He had surrendered his rent-controlled apartment near the beach in Santa Monica, and gave up his conventional life, in order to further his spiritual life. He had moved to McLeod Ganj, and planned to be there for four years.

I crossed paths with Joe several times a day. Eventually we agreed to have supper together each night, at a place called the Kunga House on Bhagsunag Road. At the time, there was a man from Connecticut, at the restaurant, who was showing the cooks how to make Italian food. He was an excellent cook, and he managed to put together some great dishes even without the usual olive oil and herbs, which were not available in North India.

Dear God, Please Change Me as Needed

My friend Joe was a practicing Buddhist, but food was his religion. He enjoyed a meal more than most, and he treated the whole experience with great reverence. One evening at about 5 pm, we were seated at the restaurant enjoying our dinner and all the good company, when another man entered the room. I called him the mountain man. Bearded and powerfully built, he was also powerfully odoriferous; it was clear he did not have access to a shower or bathtub. Joe seemed to tense up a bit when the mountain man walked in. He tensed a little more as the mountain man came over to our table. Joe was seated on my right The mountain man sat opposite Joe, one seat further to the right. He did not speak. after a moment, he reached across the empty seat, and took food off the plate of the man sitting at the table across from me.

I was very surprised at this. I assumed they must know each other, and looked for a sign that they did, but I saw no indication of it. So what was going on? Just then, Joe put down his knife and fork and folded his hands in his lap. He then closed his eyes and dropped his head to his chin. Joe just sat there, motionless. He appeared to be in some kind of meditation. After about a minute, the mountain man stopped eating. His chair scraped loudly on the hard floor as he pushed it out to get up. As he pushed the chair back in place, he slammed it against the table, then walked off and out the door. In a few seconds, Joe raised his left arm up, pulled back his sleeve with the other hand and looked at his watch.

"Fifty-two seconds," he said. "Best time yet!" My questioning look got a smile from Joe as he said, "Do you want to know what I did?"

"Yes," I said. "What ***did*** you do?"

Joe explained, "I went inside to my Buddha nature and asked to be changed as needed according to the situation at hand."

"That's it?" I asked. "Nothing else?"

"Nothing else," said Joe. Joe went on to explain that "mountain man" had been showing up at his meals over and over, uncannily sitting at his table repeatedly in more than one place in McLeod Ganj for several days. Each time he showed up, mountain man would do something rude and outrageous. "He has been serving as my mirror," explained Joe. "I don't even fully know what it's about yet, but I do not need to know any more to ask for help. That's what I did. I asked for help – in a specific way that recognizes that I am the creator of my reality, and that if I wish my reality to change, I must change. As soon as I was changed," Joe concluded, "the problem changed."

"You said this has been happening over and over?" I asked.

Joe anticipated my next question. "Yes, it has been happening over and over; this time I got rid of him in under a minute. Like I said, that was my best time yet. I will just keep at it until I understand it fully and then it will change fully."

"How do you know it will work?" I asked.

"Here's what I do know," said Joe, "The other way, where I assume the problem is outside of me, does <u>not</u> work. So I have chosen to do something different in order to get different results."

"Oh, you mean like that definition of insanity, that quote attributed to Albert Einstein?" I continued. "Insanity: doing the same thing over and over again and expecting different results."

"Exactly right," said Joe. "Exactly right." "You've got to do things differently to get different results."

You Don't Have to Take it Personally

The Bagsu Hotel I stayed at was owned by the government of Himachal Pradesh. It was adequate in every way and served my every need. My room had a wall of windows facing south, with all the mountain sunshine making the room very pleasant in the daytime. The Dalai Lama would be giving his public teachings in the coming weeks, and I had decided to stay to attend them. So much for my presentation back in New Mexico! The actual date of the teachings was a moving target. I just had to make the commitment and make the choice to stay, which I did. The event of His Holiness's teachings drew many monks from near and far. Each morning I awoke to the sound of the monks chanting in the Dalai Lama's Buddha temple, and each morning I felt a great deal of energy moving through me as a result. All combined, the events and energies that gathered in my life while I was immersed in the world of Tibetan Buddhism brought on a major spiritual cleansing in me.

Allow me to introduce you to one very powerful dude, Padmasambhava; the Indian siddha master who brought Buddhism from India to Tibet. He is also known as Guru Rinpoche; Guru meaning remover of darkness or teacher, Rinpoche meaning a fully realized master who reincarnates knowingly. He is so revered within the Tibetan tradition, that they practice something called Guru Yoga; Guru referring to Padmasambhava and Yoga meaning union with. This practice includes the chanting of the Padmasambhava mantra: Om Ah Hum Vajra Guru Padma Siddhi Hum. I had originally learned this practice from my teacher Tom Kenyon. I eagerly joined a group of a few devotees, who gathered at a hotel room in town, to practice the mantra. However after three days, schedules conflicted and we could not continue. Having started the practice, I decided to continue on my own.

Then I decided I really wanted to try it out, so the next day I did it all day long. The following day I was not well. I felt exhausted, irritable and just plain miserable. As was my mid-morning habit by now, I walked down the hill to the Dalai Lama's Buddha temple to meditate in the energy of the temple. There I sat, at the feet of the statue of Padmasambhava, feeling as if I was in an emotional meat grinder. I begged and prayed, asking everyone and anyone on the spiritual plane, for help; all the while feeling there probably was no help for me. Suddenly I heard, with a fierce clarity in my head, **"You don't have to take it personally."** I knew this message came from Guru Rinpoche. The fierceness of it felt the same as when I had done the Guru Yoga mantra all day the day before. There it was, the sage advice I had asked for and now I had to deal with it. Many years and a lot of work later, I can say I understand this much better now. As the creator of my own experience of reality, I am generating all of my own experience, the parts I like and the parts I don't like. It is never about what someone else did to me; it is always about what I did to myself, and what I have created for myself. So, all I have to do is take responsibility for my creations, then change *me* to get different results.

Now, let's see what Harry and Swami are up to.

Chapter 12
Removal of My Need to Not Know What I Love

"There is no passion to be found in settling for a life that is less than the one you are capable of living."

-Nelson Mandela

The next day, Harry rose early with a good appetite. After eating a good breakfast, he decided to go outside and enjoy the fine weather. This day there was a blue sky and a soft breeze and it was just warm enough to go walking without a jacket. As Harry walked along the paved pathway, he found himself reflecting on yesterday's success in overcoming his fear about reaching for what he would have in his life. As he walked along, it occurred to him that his choice of work was one example of hiding out, not really doing what he loved, but staying under the radar. "What do I love?" Harry asked himself. He thought of his mom, but other than that he had no answer. "I'll have to ask Swami about this," thought Harry.

Just then, Harry felt a small rush of energy in his head as he heard, "Return to your meditation chair." It was a command, but one given in the still, small voice. Harry felt a little tired at the thought of doing more work with Swami so soon after yesterday's session, but something in him knew he would do it. The time was right. He had taken a long weekend off and had the time. "Okay," Harry said to himself, "I will finish my walk and go back to work with Swami." As Harry settled into his La-Z-Boy recliner, he felt the Presence of Swami.

"Are you ready?" asked Swami.

"I guess so, if you are," replied Harry.

"I am always at your service, day or night. You need only ask," answered Swami. "What prompted this session was your realization that you do not know what you love."

"Okay," said Harry, "I get it. I did not realize you were listening to my thoughts as I walked."

“Isn’t that what I always do?” replied Swami.

“What if I *don’t* want you to listen to my thoughts?” Harry asked.

“You are certainly free to limit my access, but how would it help you to go it alone?” replied Swami.

“Okay,” said Harry, “I get it.”

“Your commitment to your spiritual path is what brought me to you,” Swami went on.

“I don’t remember ever asking for your help,” Harry interjected.

“No, you would not,” replied Swami. “Your path was set at your birth. At that time it was established that as you approached age thirty-five, your soul would begin to awaken, and then your personal development would begin.”

“Is it like that for everyone?” Harry asked.

“Some few are born in full awareness,” Swami replied, “having achieved it in a previous life. In such cases they have a mission to accomplish, beyond any additional soul evolution they achieve. Most are like you, Harry. They live a mundane life until they awaken, then their spiritual growth accelerates; just as it is now for you. Any more questions before we go on?" asked Swami.

"No, I think I'm ready," said Harry, feeling fatigued.

"Your fatigue is a sign that you have already begun your next piece of work," said Swami. "Ego resistance is a constant issue as you do your inner work."

"Why?" asked Harry.

"Your ego is a collection of reactions," Swami answered, "a collection of opinions about the realty as experienced by you. Remember, your ego is driven by survival needs. Ego thinks it is protecting you, when in fact it is limiting you. Ego is, however, very dedicated to its role as protector; it challenges anything from outside the 'safe box' it has made for itself. And so, as you approach this work on yourself, your ego may feel threatened or challenged. It is part of you, it knows what you are up to, and it can make you sleepy any time it wants. You may find it a nuisance, but you will always be able to overcome it."

As Harry took this in, he saw that his ego resistance was most certainly there, so he made a deliberate choice to go beyond it. Harry felt good about himself after he made this decision.

"Good for you," Swami encouraged. "Commitment and self-discipline are needed on the spiritual path."

"What next?" Harry asked.

"Next we will explore this business about love," said Swami. "And the fact that you do not know what you love."

"Good," said Harry. "It does seem to me that I ought to know what I love by now."

"Agreed," said Swami. "So let us begin. We will do a removal of your need to not know what you love. Hold further questions until after we do this removal," instructed Swami.

"Okay," said Harry, "you read my mind."

"Yes," said Swami. "Let us begin. **This is the removal of my *need* to not know what I love,"** Swami intoned. **"This is for Harry, ____________________ and we begin now."**

Harry felt nothing at first. Then suddenly there was a sinking feeling at his solar plexus and his stomach seemed to ache. Just as Harry was about to say something, the ache disappeared in a rush of anxiety; then suddenly Harry felt peaceful. Confused by this, Harry was again about to say something when all of a sudden he saw a mouse in his inner vision. "A mouse!?" Harry exclaimed aloud. "What could this be?" Harry wondered to himself.

"You have just met the symbol of your anxiety," said Swami. "Now you can talk with it."

"How?" asked Harry, feeling anxious for some reason.

"Put the mouse in the bubble and ask it why it is here," directed Swami.

"Okay," said Harry, "if you say so." Harry did as he was guided to do. He put the mouse in the bubble directly in front of him and then said "Okay, mouse, why are you here?"

Looking directly at Harry, the mouse said only one word. "Fear."

"Fear?" thought Harry, wondering what that could be about.

"Stay with it," urged Swami. "Ask the mouse, 'fear of what?'"

"Okay," said Harry. In his mind, Harry asked the mouse in the bubble, "Fear of what?"

"Loss," answered the mouse.

“Loss?” wondered Harry. “Loss of what?” Harry asked.

“Loss of what you love.” said the mouse.

“But I don’t even know what I love!” exclaimed Harry.

“So you are safe,” said the mouse.

“Safe? How?” wondered Harry. Just then, Harry began to see the dilemma he was in. As long as he did not know what he loved, he could never lose it.

Suddenly Harry saw the mouse in the bubble again, this time nibbling on a piece of cheese. “Why did the image change?” thought Harry. “The mouse is getting what he needs,” Harry mused to himself. “The mouse was getting what he needed, his food. “What’s my food?” wondered Harry aloud.

“Remember, the image in the bubble is an expression of you,” Swami reminded Harry.

“Oh, right!” thought Harry.

“As soon as we took out your need to ‘not know what you love,’ this vision appeared.” Swami explained. “And so you can see from the vision of the mouse with his cheese, you have already shifted this issue in you somewhat. There is more to do; are you ready to go on?" asked Swami.

"Yes, I'm ready," said Harry with a new-found confidence. "I am feeling good about this work we are doing. Thank you for your help," said Harry.

"Very well, let us continue," said Swami. **"This is the removal of my *habit* of not knowing what I love. This is for Harry, ____________________ and we begin now."**

As before, Harry became still and waited for the next thing to happen. Suddenly a light came on inside his head, and he remembered when he was ten years old and wanted new sneakers. He heard his mother's voice say, "Why are you complaining so much about not having new sneakers?" and he felt guilty at the memory of the scene. Harry also remembered how conflicted he felt, complaining that he did not have new sneakers "like all the other kids." He wanted to be cool like the other cool kids, but he did not have the money and neither did his mother.

"So you can see where this event set up a conflict in you," Swami remarked. "You really loved getting new sneakers, and this time you could not. You really loved your mother, but this time you felt let down by her."

"But it is such a petty thing!" Harry objected.

"Social pressure is a major issue in the lives of young school children in affluent cultures," said Swami. "You felt driven to be part of the 'in' crowd. You felt anxious to be accepted by your peers. You felt the need to be included; to be the same; to have cool shoes."

"Your dilemma however, was that the budget did not allow it. So, you felt let down by your mother even though you really loved her," Swami continued. "And in the end you felt conflicted; on the one hand you really loved your mother, on the other hand you really loved the idea of new sneakers, and you felt you could not have both."

"You could not have the thing you just HAD to have and you mixed that up with your love for your mother," Swami explained. "In the end, you did not know whether you really wanted your mother's love if you did not get the thing you REALLY HAD to have, the sneakers."

"Another way to say it is you did not know if you could trade feeling secure socially (having cool shoes) for your mother's love. You were 'in a bind,' you were immature, and you made the selfish choice. Not a surprise, given that you were ten years old." Swami concluded.

"You chose the sneakers, the thing you *desperately needed* (or so you thought), over your mothers' love. When you saw you would not get the sneakers anyway, you doubted your mothers' love," Swami added.

"So what now?" asked Harry.

"You have just witnessed the change we intended," Swami answered. "Remember, the visions that come to you are in response to the stated intention. This time we asked to remove your 'habit of not knowing what you love.' The conflicted feelings you had between your mother and the new sneakers symbolized all such confused feelings, and probably the root of them."

"So, my feeling that I do not know what I love came from this little event in my life?" asked Harry.

"The issue was never resolved, so it still had legs, it was still operating in you," answered Swami. "You formed a belief that you can't have what you love (the sneakers), or love what you had (your mom).

This is a painful conflict, so you hide it under some other story like 'I don't care that much about it.'"

"Okay, thanks," said Harry.

"Are you ready to proceed?" asked Swami.

"Yes," answered Harry.

"Very well," said Swami, "we will complete this topic with the removal of 'my denial that I don't know what I love'. **This is the removal of my *denial* that I don't know what I love. This is for Harry, ____________________ and we begin now."**

As before, Harry sat quietly and waited. At first he noticed a feeling in his belly, as though he was hungry. Suddenly the rumbling became very warm, and Harry felt a rush of heat through his abdomen. The heat moved up to his throat and felt warm in his neck. "What's this?" he thought to himself.

"This is the energy being released as a result of this piece of work you are doing," answered Swami. "As soon as you released the denial, the energy tied up in that denial moved. In this case, it moved very quickly."

"I did not have any visions with that removal," said Harry.

"Not to worry," Swami replied. "Your response was complete on the energetic level as you felt it move through your body. To summarize," Swami continued, "first you had the need. We don't really care what the reason was for the need. All we care about is being done with the need for the issue. So we removed it. The pattern was in place long enough to create a habit, so we took the habit out. Any time you have an unhealthy habit long enough, you tend to deny it. 'Who, me? I don't have that problem,' we say to ourselves. So you can see, in denying it we passively hold on to it. These are the steps that will allow you to remove those accumulated burdensome beliefs in your subconscious mind."

And now, we return to my personal adventure.

Chapter 13

Shiva Comes as a Cobra

"The easiest way for you to reach God at this time in history is the practice of Japa"

-Sai Baba

The Presence of the Holy Man

The term darshan means "the sight or presence of the holy man." Darshan with Sai Baba was always powerful for me. After Sai Baba became a part of my life, my inner purification deepened and accelerated. He would appear to me periodically and make a gesture with His hand that said "Come to Me." I always went. I travelled to Puttaparthi in South India to see Sai Baba at least seventeen times in fifteen years. Each visit was beneficial in its own way.

The Practice of Japa

One thing Sai Baba stressed is the practice of Japa. Japa refers to a meditation practice designed to develop focus. It is also called "repetition of the name." Whichever aspect of the Divine you focus on is your personal choice. There are three distinct parts of Japa.

1. First is the mala itself, used as counting beads.

2. Second is the name you choose for your practice. For example, I have always used the name Sai Baba for my Japa.

3. Third is the picture of the deity, which may at first be a picture you gaze at while you chant the name of this deity. *The promise is that once you have repeated the name of your meditational deity enough times, you will be gifted with an actual vision of the actual being.*

There is powerful magic in doing Japa. There is a principle of consciousness stated thus: "The name and the form are one." Based on this principle, you can see that saying the name of the deity is equal to reaching out into the cosmos and pulling them to you. They cannot fail to show up when you speak their name. That is the power of the word.

Japa brings focus to your mind. Japa gets your thought, word and action all focused on the same thing. How? The practice requires you to use all three in unison.

1. You use your mind (thought) to either look at or visualize the deity.

2. You use your word (speech) in order to repeat the name.

3. You do the action with your hand to count on the beads the repetitions of the name you use.

While doing Japa, your thought, your word and your deed are all focused on the same thing. How often does that happen in your life? For most of us, almost never. Sai Baba advised everyone to use Japa as the foundation of their spiritual practice. **Give it a try**. Who knows what you have attained in other incarnations? Your practice of Japa just may tap into some powerful personal spiritual attainments from before you got to this life.

Stay With the Name You Choose

One other aspect of Japa stressed by Sai Baba has to do with the name you choose to use.

Whatever name you choose, stay with it. Staying with the same name deepens your connection to the being involved. It is the depth you develop that brings the attainments in consciousness. If you switch around from one name to another, you dilute your experience. Switching around works against you; stay focused and let the practice of Japa work for you.

Help Ever, Hurt Never

Another thing Sai Baba stressed is selfless service. This means serving the well-being of others. This does not mean you should burn yourself out helping others. There must be balance in your life in order for you to serve well over time. You must take care of your own needs in order to be truly available to serve the well-being of others. A teaching I received at Unity of Sedona applies very well to this topic: God first, self second, others third. If you go in this order, you will do well yourself, and you will also sometimes be in a position to help others do well through your service.

I continued to visit Sai Baba regularly, slightly more often than once a year. The trip was long, good for burning off negative karma. Three days of travel to get to the ashram in southern India, then darshan twice a day for nine days, then two days to get back home to the States became a routine. While crossing the International Date Line made the outbound trip longer, in calendar time it was always two flights of nine to ten hours each, with an overnight in Frankfurt, Germany. This was my routine through the 1990s until I got to 1999. Then the next thing happened.

Ganesha – Remover of Obstacles

I came to know that I could have the help of a deity called Ganesha. Ganesha is the wisdom aspect of the Divine. What the "wisdom aspect" means to me is this: rather than seeing obstacles as insurmountable problems, the wisdom aspect (Ganesha) will take a look from a different angle, a different perspective, in order to see the situation differently. It could be as simple as standing to the left a couple of feet and taking another look. A petition to Ganesha (your own wisdom aspect) will always help. In India, Ganesha temples are found everywhere, even out in the countryside. The devout start every day, indeed every project, with a puja to Ganesha.

I decided I would look for a small statue of Ganesha to keep on my altar at home. In searching for a suitable piece, I learned that there are Ganesha statues with his trunk to the right and others with his trunk to the left. While the left trunk indicated spiritual matters, the right trunk indicated physical, temporal matters. I decided I needed a right-trunk Ganesha and began shopping for one. Eventually I found myself walking into Aftab's shop. My attitude at the time, was that I would "not allow these Kashmiri shopkeepers to take advantage of me." Sitting at the counter at Aftab's shop in Whitefield (the location of another Sai Baba ashram), I told him what I wanted and he began showing me different pieces. Nothing he showed me looked right for me, and I was getting discouraged about it. Aftab then reached into some invisible corner and pulled out a small silver Ganesha. We bargained, and I came to what I would make as my final offer of $100 for the piece. I told him that was all I would pay, that was my limit.

Aftab sat back, looked at me and slowly asked, "So, it is all you will pay for this Ganesha?"

"Yes," I said firmly. "That is my limit."

At that, Aftab placed the small statue in front of me and said, "It is yours." I was surprised and delighted that I had gotten the piece at what I thought was a good price.

Our business concluded, Aftab became animated and said to me, "Do you want to know what I planned to get for the piece?"

"Okay," I said. "How much did you plan to get?"

With a joyful and smiling face, Aftab announced that He had planned to sell the piece for $260, and that he had paid half that. Now the energy I felt with Aftab was very easy and relaxed, so I asked him where the piece had come from. "Rishikesh," answered Aftab. He went on to say: "Once a year I travel to my home in Srinagar, Kashmir, to visit my family, then I travel around the Himalayan region to buy things for my shop. This small Ganesha that you have bought came from my last trip to Rishikesh. I have bargained with the man who sold it to me for the last two years. The man did not want to sell it, but this year he did. It was for you."

In the coming years I got to know Aftab and found him to be a very spiritual man. He personally sponsored the education of poor children from the lowest classes in the village. He was generous and kind, as well as a good businessman. He had sold the small silver Ganesha to me because he knew I needed it for some reason. Within days, I found out why.

The Ganges River

Hearing the name Rishikesh did something to me. I felt an attraction I did not understand and knew I had to go there. I had heard of the Ganges River that flowed down out of the Himalayas and then southwest to Varanasi, and finally reached the sea at the Bay of Bengal in Bangladesh. Rishikesh is well known as a place of purification for devotional people. Indian families would make the journey when they could; such a pilgrimage to a holy place for spiritual purposes is known as a Yatra. The ghats (beaches, or places you can enter the river) along the Ganges River are well attended by devotional people. When you are there by the river in Rishikesh, you see the "Holy dip" performed throughout the day in many places.

Off I went again on another unplanned Yatra! After one more flight to Delhi from Bangalore and another long cab ride to Rishikesh, I arrived in town in the middle of the day. I knew I wanted to check out the Ganges River, so I asked my cab driver to take me to a hotel as close to the river as possible. He dropped me off at a hotel called Baseraa Hotel. Funny thing about that is baseraa means hotel, therefore I stayed at the 'Hotel' hotel. It was about a three minute walk from my room to Triveni Ghat (three rivers beach). The Three Rivers that meet at this spot are the Ganges River, the Yamuna River and the Sarasvati River.

After checking into my hotel, I walked down to the Ganges river to check it out. The gate to the stone-paved plaza area was broken and I could see from the droppings that the cows had been allowed to roam at will. Standing next to the Ganges River, I went to the devotional place within me and just waited. Soon I felt called to walk into the river. The main current was very strong as the river was more than a hundred yards across. Standing in the river water up to my knees, I watched a couple of kids at play. I kept to the calm waters near the shore. I just stood there and waited to see what would happen next. In my inner vision, I suddenly saw a female figure rise up out of the river, just in front of me. I felt welcomed by Her as she greeted me with great Love. She made a gesture with her left arm, directing my attention to the river water itself. "Be bathed," she seemed to say. "Be Blessed," as her image faded. This was a wonderful welcome! As I walked back onto the beach I thought, "I must do something to deepen my connection to this river!" I went back to my hotel to rest for the afternoon, before I returned to the river. Back at the Ganges that evening, I was delighted to find that a small group of local people had set up their altar for a puja of some kind. It was the evening Aarti (prayers) to Mother Ganga, and it was a great gift to me. The devotional quality of the local participants was very high. I later learned that this group, all men from the area, had brought about a resurgence of devotional practice for Maa Ganga by reinstituting the ancient Vedic practice of singing the evening Aarti to Her.

Light poured from the eyes of the wiry old man in a simple cotton dhoti (a skirt like cotton cloth wrapped around the waist) as he sang the Aarti and poured the blessing of the river water over my head. I returned each evening for a total of nine nights, to receive this blessing. After my first Maa Ganga Aarti, I walked back to my room, showered and went to bed. Sleep was not meant to be. I lay there on the bed, sweating a thick layer of I don't know what. I could scrape it off my skin with my fingernails, I could wash it off in the shower, but as long as I was in bed I oozed a thick sweat all night and all day. I did not feel rested in the morning, so I stayed in bed. The ooze continued as long as I was in the room. When I got up and went outside for some food, the thick sweat would stop and my energy level returned. As soon as I got back to the room, it resumed. This went on for nine days and nights.

Kedarnath

During the seventh day of my purification with Mother Ganga, I ran out of rupees. Accordingly, I had to find a place to change dollars into rupees. At that time in Rishikesh, you could not just go to the ATM. I walked for about twenty minutes into Rishikesh. I finally saw a sign on a building for a travel agent called Mahamaya Travels, where I could change dollars into rupees. I went in. Chandra Prakash spoke fluent English, this was welcome to me! He was happy to sit and talk, so we did, for an hour or more. He explained to me how he was a devout man, but a busy man, so he hired a priest in Rishikesh to do prayers for him. Later I learned this is a normal, ancient practice in much of India.

A poster on his office wall drew my attention and I repeatedly turned to look at it, almost against my will. Chandra couldn't help but notice this, so he told me about the place on the poster. "It is called Kedarnath,"

Chandra told me. “It is the oldest Temple dedicated to Lord Shiva, in the Himalaya.” He went on, saying that Kedarnath means “the place of Kedar.” Kedar (Lord of the Mountains) is one of the names for Shiva, the destroyer aspect of the Hindu trinity. I was intrigued, but I did not want to be sold anything, so I said goodbye and made my way back to my hotel. I had had enough of the oozy sweat for that day, so I went for a meal and then directly to Triveni Ghat to be early for the Ganga Aarti.

Back at the Aarti that night, I had a clear knowing that I would go to Kedarnath, high up in the mountains, to visit the Shiva temple there. So, the next day I returned to Mahamaya Tours and Travels and asked Chandra to arrange the trip. I had been told in meditation that I was to stay there three full nights and days, which meant one day to get up to the temple, three nights and days in the high mountain valley and another day to get back down. My travel arrangements were made accordingly. My guide was a young man called Arun. He was well educated, being from a Brahmin family. He had taught himself to read English with two newspapers, one in English and one in his own language. He was a very intelligent young man who aimed to please, and we got along well. The cab ride from Rishikesh to Gauri Kund took fourteen hours, including stops. Gauri Kund (elevation 5,946 feet) is a Hindu pilgrimage site and base camp for the trek to Kedarnath Temple, in Uttaranchal, India. The Kedarnath temple complex sits in a high mountain valley (elevation 11,755 feet) with a backdrop of the snow-covered Kedarnath Mountains.

It was in September of 1999 that I found myself on the back of a donkey, riding the steep inclines of the trek up to the Kedarnath Temple complex. The spray from the rushing river filled the air, and everything on the trail was damp and slippery. The "saddle" on the donkey was a single layer of leather over a molded steel plate, and I knew I was in trouble! Half way up to the temple took about two hours. Here we stopped for the donkeys to rest and eat. That was all the donkey riding time I needed to become sore beyond description. All I could do was grin and bear it. Another two hours in the saddle and we arrived at the temple complex about dusk. My guide escorted me to find my lodging.

As I approached my hotel, I was met by a young man in white robes who introduced himself by his full four part Sanskrit name, none of which I could pronounce. In the end he said "You can call me Dave". I came to think of him as the "young priest."

Dave's English was very good, and he asked if I was there for puja. I said I was not sure why I was there, but sure, let's do puja. I really did not know what to expect, when the next day, my guide came to my room to tell me the priests had arrived to escort me to the temple.

All four of us arrived at the temple and entered the inner sanctum, in the middle of which, stands a large granite rock protruding from the earth. This stone is said to be the one that the Indian master Adi Shankaracharya raised for the Pandava brothers after the battle of Kurukshetra. The story goes that Arjuna and the rest of the Pandava brothers had journeyed to this spot in the mountains after the battle of Kurukshetra (As described in the Mahabarata). They were feeling despondent after having had to do battle with their friends and relatives, most of whom they had killed. Adi Shankaracharya met the brothers at this spot, tapped the Earth with his staff, and a large, knobbed stone of granite rose up from the ground. Shankaracharya instructed the brothers to do puja to Lord Shiva at this spot as a means to assuage their grief. The temple itself was constructed around the stone raised by Shankaracharya. The current temple is estimated to be between 1000 and 3000 years old.

It is buried every year in forty feet of snow. In 2013, the temple withstood violent flooding that badly damaged the surrounding town. The temple was protected by a big boulder that forced the floodwaters to take a route around the temple. The temple survived, the town did not.

Om Nama Shivaya

There we were, the four of us seated on the floor along the back edge of the Shiva Lingam, inside the temple at Kadarnath. The wise old priest, leading the puja, was named Sudarshan; I came to think of him as the old priest. Just as the old priest was getting ready to begin, I heard Shiva say clearly in my head, "If you pray to me, I will make you my son."

I thought, "Good – how do I do that?" I asked my guide, who was seated to my left. He translated and passed my question on to the young priest who was seated to his left. He then passed my question on to the old priest who sat at the end of the line. After a brief discussion, the old priest gave the instruction to the young priest who passed it on to my guide, who translated and passed it on to me. The instruction to me was "Repeat the Shiva mantra."

I looked at my guide and said, “What mantra?” He stared at me with a baffled look of disbelief, and then passed my question up the line to the young priest. His surprised look had me wondering what was going on as he passed my question on to the old priest at the end of the line. The old priest shook his head in wonderment, and then he gave his answer to the young priest. Back down the line it came, and my guide gave me the answer. “Om Nama Shivaya.” Apparently, the priests assumed I would know which mantra to use in Shiva’s temple. While I had heard it before, I had never practiced it, at least not in this life.

I then began chanting "Om Nama Shivaya." The old priest sent the massage down the line that I should chant silently, so he could concentrate on reading the sutras (scriptures) that he was chanting. The mantra “Om Nama Shivaya,” which I began chanting that morning at Kadarnath, continued at the rate of about one repetition per second for the rest of the time I was there. I could not stop, day or night. It was less the case that I was doing the mantra, more the case that the mantra was doing me! It continued for the rest of that trip in India. After leaving Kedarnath, I returned to Puttaparthi where I stayed in a hotel near Sai Baba’s ashram. I stayed for the next two months, all the while the mantra repeated itself about once every two seconds. I would fall asleep with it going in my mind; I would wake up with it going in my mind. There was no stopping it.

Shiva Comes as a Cobra

That night, in my room at the lodging house near the Kedarnath Temple, I was unable to sleep. About two in the morning, there was a sudden intensity in the subtle energy field of my room and I came instantly alert. I could just hear the soft scraping sound as something passed under the door; there was a two-inch gap under the heavy wooden door to my room. My room was completely dark. Just then, the sense of a presence in the room was amplified by a soft scraping sound at a small table on the opposite wall. Next I heard things being moved around on the table. Then suddenly, the coconut, used in the Shiva Temple puja that morning, rolled off the table and hit the floor with a loud CRASH! In order for the coconut to roll off the table, the coconut, which was sitting in a metal tray at the back of the table, had to have been maneuvered out of the tray and around the other stuff on the table. It was being moved by…??? After it crashed to the floor, it was then rolled all the way across the floor, where it bumped into the heavy wooden door. Next, I heard the sound of the coconut being grappled, then a moment of silence as it was lifted up, then WHAM! WHAM! WHAM! The coconut was smashed against the wooden door three times. I was scared shitless! The pounding on the door stopped for a long moment, then WHAM! WHAM! WHAM! as the coconut was smashed against the door again. Silence, then a third time it happened, WHAM! WHAM! WHAM! Finally, the coconut dropped to the floor, and then the sound of soft scraping once again as something left through the gap under the door. The energy in the room dropped at the same time. Covered in sweat, my heart pounding ... What was that!

The next morning, the two priests came to my room, observed the situation and they pointed out the fang marks in the coconut made by a cobra. Overwhelmed, I was slow to grasp what was being implied, and my interpreter was not talking. It was all very intimidating to me. Then the priest suggested we do another puja in another temple. I said okay. I was here for the whole experience...whatever that was! After my guide and I had some morning tea, it was time to do the next puja.

That night, as much as I needed to rest, I was afraid to go to bed; but then what were the odds...? A second coconut, from the second puja was in a plastic bag tied in a knot, placed once again on the table against the wall. Once again, at about 2 am, I heard the now familiar soft scraping sound under the door. My heart was in my mouth! The next sound was of something sliding over the edge of the table. Then I heard the plastic bag being ripped open. Again, the coconut rolled off the table and crashed to the floor! It was rolled to the door and smashed into it repeatedly, just like the night before. This time I knew something of what was happening. I was not afraid of Shiva, but the latent fear in me was so activated that I could hardly move.

Next morning, I saw that the plastic bag had been ripped open around the coconut, like a nest, and just left in place. The door-banging coconut was on the floor and had been partly broken through. The priests came again that morning and saw what Shiva had left behind. The young priest said to me "You should stay here in Kedarnath!" Apparently, this was his idea of fun!

"Bullshit," I thought. "I'm outta here after three days." Lucky for me, there were no more pujas that day. However, I did think hard about what Shiva wanted; it seemed obvious that He was after the coconut. What were the odds that Shiva would return for a third night in a row? I did not know, but I wasn't going to take any chances! So, I cut the coconut into wedges for Shiva, just in case. I made sure that the slices would fit under the heavy wooden door to my room, so that He could take my offering. Then I cleared off the table and turned it into an altar. I placed a picture of Shiva, Parvathi and Ganesha on the table with two wedges of coconut in front.

It happened again. At about 2 am, in comes Shiva, slithering across the floor and up to the altar. Next I heard the sound of the coconut wedges being picked up, carried across the floor and then being dragged one at a time, under the door. No pounding this time! What a relief! I lay there quietly as all was still for about ten minutes. Suddenly, I had a very strong vision of Ganesha. This was followed by more sounds, unfamiliar, at the table. Now What! Less fearful now than I had been, I finally overcame it and turned on the flashlight. Nothing remained to be seen, except that the coconut wedges were gone from the altar.

The next morning, as I was at the bathroom sink, I looked out the window and saw two crows on the light pole, just outside my window. They were eating the coconut wedges I had cut for Shiva. When the priests came in that morning, they identified the droppings left behind on my altar, as being those from a mouse. I knew the mouse to be the vehicle for Ganesha.

I later told this story to my teacher Tom Kenyon, and asked his opinion about it. He said it was clear to him that I had been accepted by both Shiva and Ganesha, but he had no idea what it meant otherwise. Tom then said with a laugh, "But I would fasten my seat belt, if I were you!" I came to realize what it meant... nine years of intense purification followed; as both Shiva and Ganesha are removers of obstacles and destroyers of untruth.

About Shiva – *One way to understand Shiva is to understand the individual parts of His mantra. Na, Ma, Shi, Va, Ya are the sounds for the five elements – earth, water, air, fire, and akash (space). As such, Shiva IS the five elements of creation. These five elements are the first expressions of form. The consciousness which IS each of these elements, combines in many ways to create all the forms we see and experience. For Shiva to appear as a cobra or as a crow or as anything else is a normal part of being Shiva.*

Atmic Awareness

After three full nights and days at Kedarnath, I was more than ready to leave. I was fried! SO MUCH had happened, I was going to need some time to process it all. After our trek on foot down the mountain, my guide and I found our cab waiting for us at Gory Kund. We set off in the cab but were soon stopped by a washed-out bridge. It was just as well. My guide found me a very comfortable, clean and dry room in a guest house close to where we had been forced to stop. Exhausted, I slept for about twelve hours but it was not enough. I still felt overwhelmed, and the Shiva mantra was still running in my mind, day and night. Clearly, Shiva was having his way with me. I decided to return to Sai Baba at Puttaparthi in south India. It is a good thing I did, as I was in a state of overwhelm for about five weeks after my encounter with Shiva at Kedarnath. It took that long before I was ready for the discipline of the early 4 am lines to go into darshan with Baba.

Once I had the five weeks to integrate my experience with Shiva, I resumed the discipline of darshan. I made the early lines by 4 am each day; I was hungry for Baba's blessings. It was now the middle of November in 1999 and I had one more week before I was to return to the States. During that week, I received the blessing that my time with Shiva had prepared me for. Sai Baba regularly made eye contact with those in attendance at darshan, and He always gave me a glimpse as he walked by. Eye contact with Sai Baba was always at His option, and it could change you on the spot. This day was no different. During morning Darshan that day, Sai Baba first looked me directly in the eyes for a long couple of seconds. His glance continued through the crowd and then returned to me for a second time, and then again a third time, each time for a couple of seconds. The fourth time, when Baba looked directly into my eyes I was consumed by a vision of myself as the Atmic Light! I saw the effulgence that Sai Baba had often spoken of and written of, and it was me, sitting on the floor in the darshan hall! I knew I was the Light, and it was thrilling!

My first thought was gratitude that Sai Baba had given me the Atmic experience. My second thought was, "Well, that'll probably never happen again." Talk about missing the point! But I did not catch my error at the time.

The afternoon darshan that day, proved me very wrong. Again Sai Baba held my eyes for a couple of seconds as he approached the area I sat in, then again, and again, then once more. Was I surprised when once more I experienced myself as the Atmic Effulgence! I became a brilliant column of Light for a couple of seconds. I realized how wrong I had been to think it would probably never happen again. Sai Baba's teaching has always included the idea that Who We Are is nothing less than the Atmic Presence, the Divine Presence, the I Am Presence. We are God in a body, and nothing less. I floated out of the darshan hall that afternoon, feeling that I had just received the greatest gift of my lifetime!

The End

www.ingramcontent.com/pod-product-compliance
Lightning Source LLC
LaVergne TN
LVHW021456080426
835509LV00018B/2304